Innovation, Technology, and Finance

Innovation, Technology, and Finance

edited by
Arnold Heertje

Contributors

Patrick Artus
Angel Berges
Christian de Boissieu
Giovanni Dosi
Chris Freeman
Arnold Heertje
John Kneeshaw
Helmut Mayer
Luigi Orsenigo
Frits Prakke
José Viñals

Preface by Ernst-Günther Bröder

Basil Blackwell
for the European Investment Bank

Copyright © European Investment Bank 1988

First published 1988

Basil Blackwell Ltd
108 Cowley Road, Oxford, OX4 1JF, UK

Basil Blackwell, Inc.
432 Park Avenue South, Suite 1503
New York, NY 10016, USA

British Library Cataloguing in Publication Data
Innovation, technology, and finance.
  1. Finance. Innovation
  I. Heertje, Arnold
  332

    ISBN 0–631–15952–5

Library of Congress Cataloging in Publication Data
Innovation, technology, and finance.
    1. Technological innovations—Economic aspects.
  2. Finance. 1. Heertje, Arnold, 1934–
  HC79.T41553 1988   332.7   88–10391
  ISBN 0–631–15952–5

Typeset in 11 on 12 pt Sabon
by Photo·graphics, Honiton, Devon
Printed in Great Britain by Billing & Sons Ltd, Worcester

Contents

Preface

To mark the thirtieth anniversary of the European Investment Bank, the Bank's Management Committee decided to commission a set of essays on the economics of technological and financial innovation from leading European specialists in these fields.

The subject area is one in which the Bank itself has a keen interest, for, as part of its role in contributing to the balanced development of the Community it is closely involved in the promotion and management of change. In particular, since technological innovation is fundamental to the competitiveness of European industry, the EIB puts special emphasis on advanced technology in the long term Community investment which it helps to finance. The importance of this can only increase as progress towards the single European market gathers momentum.

Since the Bank is active in financial and non-financial markets more or less constantly, it has to keep these markets under continuous review. Scientific studies of the dynamics of innovation in these markets then complement our daily work.

The objective therefore was to obtain a series of up-to-date reviews which would give fresh perspectives and be accessible to those with a background in economics and finance who were not themselves necessarily specialists in this particular subject area. The authors were given full academic freedom of expression and they responded by providing an informed and stimulating set of papers. I would like to express my appreciation to the authors for their fine work.

Professor Heertje has kindly edited the papers for publication in this book. The Bank is publishing it to promote discussion and encourage further analytical effort in this difficult field.

Ernst-Günther Bröder

1

Technical and Financial Innovation

Arnold Heertje

Without technical and financial innovation, the economic scene offers nothing but an uninteresting, foreseeable reproduction of goods, services and financial and material means of production. The wants of consumers, as well as the products and the methods of production, tend to be unalterable. The original factors of production, nature and labour, have the same appearance over time and do not reflect any qualitative change. The process of capital formation is an endless repetition along the lines of the savings–investment mechanism, known since the days of Robinson Crusoe. In such a world, devoid of innovation, equipment that has reached the end of its useful life will be replaced by new but otherwise identical equipment.

Within a market system, transactions are based on property rights and the allocation of resources and products takes place in markets with perfect or imperfect competition. Consumers and producers behave according to the principles of the neoclassical equilibrium theory. In other words, they maximize individual utility and profit in an environment of perfect knowledge, perfect foresight, certainty and efficiency. Market failures do occur, owing to the existence of pure public goods, imperfect competition and external effects of production and consumption. They may evoke a more or less far-reaching role of the government, depending on value judgements and the comparison of costs and benefits of private and public regulation.

In the economy there is no basic difference between civil servants and entrepreneurs, although their roles in society bring about a different specification of individual targets. The static character of the economic system enables the straightforward application of the Paretian welfare theory and the rules for optimal allocation of means of production and consumer goods. Deviations from a Pareto-optimum can be established and their welfare effects can be analysed, both in a private and a public context. With a given technology the analysis leads to clear-cut results which serve as building blocks for policy recommendations. At the macro-economic level, the growth of the economy is determined by capital formation and increase in population. Economic growth is compatible with a permanent state of full-employment, if prices are flexible and if the given technology allows for substitution between labour and capital.

If the growth rate of population is far above the growth rate of capital, stagnation may emerge. By making use of comparative advantages in international trade, the drawbacks of stagnation can partly be wiped out.

Without technical and financial innovation, economic activity can be measured in an unambiguous way, as may be seen from the calculation of labour productivity. In those circumstances the unofficial economy, the complement or counterpart of the official economy, which is defined by the statistical description of the open network of economic transactions, is a straightforward collection of officially unknown transactions. Finally, a clear-cut distinction can be made between economic consequences and non-economic causes, for example, between the level of production and the psychology of the labour force.

1   INNOVATION

Innovation, in general, refers to all kinds of new developments. In the context of this book, the term denotes new developments in the field of technology and financial instruments. The term innovation is used, in particular, to indicate the introduction and application of new methods of production and new products – technical innovation – and of financial instruments which also change the financial structure – financial innovation. Innovations may have a spectacular, discontinuous and fundamental character, but this is by no means the rule. Within the technological and financial sphere, minor improvements may change the economic picture on a daily basis.

Innovation must be clearly distinguished from two other aspects of technical and financial change, viz. invention and diffusion. Invention refers to knowledge about new technical and financial possibilities. The development of technical knowledge involves developing new products and new methods of production. With regard to the financial sphere, the development of new financial instruments is at stake. The distinction between the diffusion of inventions and the diffusion of innovations should be emphasized.

The spread of knowledge about new products, new methods of production and new financial instruments is a diffusion process that is different in nature from the diffusion of newly available knowledge in the form of concrete applications, the new technology being embodied in new capital goods and products. The diffusion of knowledge through education is a useful means of promoting the economic strength of society, but it is only part of the story. Economic growth, in a quantitative and qualitative sense, requires that there be no artificial hindrance to the diffusion of innovations across firms, sectors and countries.

In reality there is a complex and interrelated network of relationships between invention, diffusion and innovation. A long time may elapse before an original, unstructured idea results in a large-scale and widespread commercial use of new products or techniques. Just how long and how complicated it will be will depend on the allocation of scarce resources and thus on economic considerations, including decisions about the final level and character of the inventive activity, the set of new possibilities and the speed of diffusion of both inventions and innovations. From this, it follows that policies can be devised that strongly influence the direction of the innovative process at large. In other words, if technical and financial change are, at least partly, determined endogenously by the economic process, there is a prima facie case for active policy-making in this area.

2　A CHANGING WORLD

With innovation the dull world of monotonous reproduction disappears. In its place is a scene in which economic agents

nervously experiment, take permanent risks and have to cope
with unforeseen problems. The increasing knowledge about new
technologies and financial instruments is dispersed and the new
possibilities are reflected in new products, methods of production
and financial structures. Due to the new products available in
the technological and financial sphere, the preferences of consumers and users of financial instruments are changing over time.
Firms no longer produce in order to satisfy the existing needs of
consumers; they are able to influence the preferences of consumers
by their strategies with respect to inventive and innovative
activities. The changes in technology may have a direct impact
on a particular firm and an indirect effect on other firms and
industries.

A diffusion process that destroys old structures takes shape,
giving rise to new economic and social conditions. The new
economic and social environment, in turn, provokes new technological breakthroughs. Technical change is neither reversible
nor divisible and it has a cumulative character. It produces
heterogeneous economies of scale and scope and a wide variety
of positive and negative external effects.

Changes in technology modify the factors of production
and their relationship to production. Technical change makes
particular capital goods obsolete and certain labour skills out of
date. It provokes a demand for new capital goods which embody
the most recent technology, and it also creates a demand for new
jobs. Technology changes the quality of labour and the quality
of labour in turn influences the state of technology. The process
of capital formation is influenced by financial innovation and the
use of natural resources partly depends on the available technology. New capital goods are the vehicle for the diffusion of
the application of new methods of production, and new methods
of production attract new investment. The process of economic
growth is a melting-pot of changes in technology, investment in
human capital and capital goods, and entrepreneurial activity.

The market is no longer just an institution for the static
allocation of resources, but a mechanism for the discovery of
new wants, new products and new methods of production.
Entrepreneurs, on the look-out for profitable ventures, are making
discoveries while chasing one another in a world of uncertainty,

imperfect knowledge and risk. Dynamic allocation of resources differs from static allocation, the latter being directed at existing needs. It is the efficiency of the process of discovery that matters. There are dynamic market failures due to technical change, and technical change is a source of dynamic X-inefficiency.

Consumer preferences are not unalterable, but can be influenced by the development of new products and consequently by technical change. To a certain extent, the direction and time path of technology is also determined by consumer preferences. As the relationship between technical and economic change is not linear but circular, we are forced to substitute the neoclassical scheme of analysis for a more evolutionary approach of which a historical framework is an essential feature. Entrepreneurs react to uncertainty and imperfect knowledge; they learn from experience and search for new possibilities.

From a welfare point of view, it is necessary to weigh up the welfare of present and future generations. However, this cannot be done on the basis of the Paretian welfare theory. Market structures can no longer be ranked on the basis of the static optimal allocation of resources; the mutual relationship between technical change and market structure necessitates a simultaneous explanation of both. In the market strategy the emphasis has shifted from price competition to 'non-price competition'. Against a background of ever-changing products and methods of production the supply side plays the major role and the demand side the minor role on the market and in production. In the short run, surpluses and shortages of capital goods, labour and final products emerge as a consequence of technical change, X-inefficiency and rigidity. The informal economy is partly caused by these stocks of goods and labour, which are increasingly characteristic of the formal economy. The decisions society takes with regard to the levels of income and wages determine the choice and diffusion of techniques, resulting in even more surpluses and shortages of labour. In short, the analysis of economic reality enforces us to study situations of disequilibrium.

Since the influence of technical change on an economy is to bring about a continuous stream of exogenous shocks and unforeseen events, the application of static Paretian welfare theory gives rise to several major problems. As technology influences

Arnold Heertje

consumer preferences, the application of the criterion of Pareto in order to evaluate and rank technology-led changes in welfare runs into a peculiar chicken and egg reasoning. To apply the criterion of Pareto, one has to start from given consumer preferences, but the product innovation to be evaluated itself modifies those preferences.

A second problem concerns the interpretation of optimal allocations in view of technical change. It is no longer the static conception of the market but the dynamic efficiency of the market mechanism that matters. Under these circumstances, judgements on the basis of welfare economics demand the weighing up of the welfare of present and future generations. This takes us outside the scope of static Paretian welfare theory. One gets a glimpse of the problems that may arise by regarding the mutual relationship of technical change and market structures. Schumpeter's positive attitude with respect to monopolistic practices is based on his assumption that the fruits of innovation will go to society at large and to its members. Yet a more sophisticated welfare theoretical argument is needed to put Schumpeter's vision in a theoretical perspective.

At the macro-economic level technical change causes cyclical growth of a heterogeneous nature in which disequilibrium is the rule and equilibrium the exception. The process of economic growth runs by fits and starts, due to the fact that consumers, entrepreneurs and labourers lack flexibility and the capacity to make adjustments. Other causes are the barriers to entry to markets and the heterogeneity of products and methods of production with regard to costs and commercial possibilities. Once the diffusion of technical innovations starts, the cumulative character and the increasing returns to scale of innovations make for an impressive upswing of the business cycle. On the labour market major quantitative and qualitative changes take place. The structure of production changes dramatically over time as new productive activities come to the fore and old ones are swept away. Many new – often small – firms enter the market, sometimes independent of big firms, but often also as satellites of large multinationals. These features of economic development are even more pronounced if efficient ways of financing the innovative process are available and even more so if, at the same time, financial innovation that stimulates the process of capital formation takes place. In particular, if the new technology is embodied in new capital goods and if new products demand major changes in production, the process of investment must be at the centre of attention, in the sphere of both economic analysis and economic policy.

3   MARKETS AND COMPLEMENTARY ASSETS

The development of new technical insights and financial instruments is one thing, their successful application within the context of a dynamic market economy is quite another matter. It has been shown that the companies or institutions that discover new products, methods of production or financial mechanisms, do not necessarily benefit the most. Economic reality provides many examples of the opposite situation, in which imitators seem to get hold of the big profits. The development of this theory in the recent literature (Teece, 1986) deserves to be mentioned here, as it is of the utmost importance for the process of investment and for the diffusion of the applications of new technology.

Let us assume that several well-known European pharmaceutical firms are trying to discover a drug to combat the disease AIDS. In view of the great significance of this product, high expectations as to the profits are at stake and thus substantial sums are being invested. One day, as a side-result, firm A discovers a product which, within the European community, appears to be very useful in the veterinary and agricultural field. Firm A brings the product to the market, but does not possess the fine-tuned computer-controlled machinery to produce the product in an efficient way. Additionally, the firm lacks the distribution channels to market the product effectively. Other, competitive firms in the industry become aware of the product and prove to be able to produce it in a different but fully acceptable way. Thanks to their efficient and advanced methods of production, they have an entry to the world of veterinarians which may last for years. Ultimately, the big profits are not made by firm A, who discovered the product, but by the imitating firms, who are the followers in the market, both in the technical and commercial sense.

Teece developed a theory to explain the chain of events just described. If patents do not effectively protect new technologies, so that they can be taken over quite easily, the dynamic outcome of the market process largely depends on the question of which company has the proper set of complementary assets to market the innovation successfully. These complementary assets may be commercial capacities, production facilities, financial advantages or other assets, missing links of which the firms were not aware. As this set of complementary assets is, in principle, independent of the often unforeseen innovation, it may be only by chance that the firm who made the innovation possesses the optimal mix. This line of reasoning may explain why many innovative firms disappear from the market, after having initially experienced success. The theory also demonstrates the conditions under which firms are prepared to tie in to other firms outside their own industry. They are willing to arrange for joint ventures, mostly on a temporary basis. Recent developments indicate that even multinationals, operating in world markets, do change partners from time to time in order to be able to cope with new competitive challenges. Teece's theory may also throw new light on the continuing discussion of whether small or large firms contribute most to innovation and technical change. The size of the firm as such is not decisive, but it is of vital concern whether the firm possesses a set of complementary commercial, financial and organizational assets compatible with the product or process innovation. Since a regular stream of product innovations, spread across sectors, industries and firms, is combined with a permanently changing composition of complementary assets, economic life, in which technical and financial innovation play important roles, is characterized by the surprising successes and unexpected failures of certain firms. Teece's theory is relevant to every firm whenever it has an innovative idea; it is essential that the management asks itself the following question: Do we possess the set of complementary assets necessary to translate a technical breakthrough into a commercial success, and which strategy must we follow if that is not entirely the case? It would be going too far to relate dynamic X-inefficiency exclusively to management failures, for apart from the unforeseen character of many technical and financial innovations, it is also hard to predict which complementary assets are needed to be successful in the market. In many cases, however, major mistakes in management can be detected: for example, during the development of a new product, it may have been overlooked that distribution channels are needed in order to market that product.

4 EUROPEAN ECONOMY AND COMPLEMENTARY ASSETS

The lack of complementary assets may explain why imitating firms are often commercially more successful than the original innovative firms. This idea may be generalized in order to explain the increasingly observable fact that European economies show a striking difference between potential and actual use of existing technological knowledge and possibilities. There is an enormous disparity between the level of technology that is applied, both in the private and the public sector, and the level of technology that is attainable. As long as investment is relatively low, it is hardly to be expected that this technology-gap will be reduced. To stimulate growth in our economies, a substantial investment plan has to be carried out which, in turn, would also raise the actual level of technology. The interaction of technological and financial innovation and investment could provoke much higher growth rates in the European community than we experience at present.

Why is Europe so far behind Japan and the US with regard to the diffusion of applications of new technology in all sectors of the economy (Morishima, 1982)? From the analysis of the complementary assets needed to bring innovations into practice at the firm's level on a very profitable basis a suggestion may be derived for the economy at large. The lack of a modern infrastructure, necessary in order to carry out major innovations in the private and public sector, may be one missing complementary asset. The lack of civil servants prepared to take risks in the field of bureaucracy may hamper the implementation of new technologies, particularly in the small-business sector of the economy. The lack of coordination between the different departments of the public sector may slow down the diffusion of information technology within that sector. If no venture capital market is available, many possible technical breakthroughs are forced to die before they have a chance to prove their commercial profitability. And, of course, the lack of a European market is a bottleneck in the development of new products and the application of new methods of production in the European community.

Hence the fact that new technology is available by no means guarantees the application of new technical possibilities on a large scale. On the contrary, one gets the impression that there is a strong tendency to stick to old procedures, old institutions, old methods of decision-making, old human relations and, consequently, old products and methods of production.

Society seems to have great difficulty in finding the optimal mix between the new potentialities, provided by technological and financial innovation, and the necessary complementary changes in institutional and political organization. Our policy-makers must therefore shift their attention from the technologies as such, to the social, economic and political conditions that favour the implementation of the new technical and financial possibilities. An investment policy without such a broad social scope will prove to be ineffective. The shift of emphasis of technology policy from the promotion of research and development (R & D) to the active stimulation of the diffusion of applications of advanced technology, is essential for the creation of a more efficient and more humane society in the next decade. This is no more than the mirror-image of the insight that the analysis of changes in institutions is important if the social institutional framework is to be more than a passive framework (Soete, 1986). In Europe economic growth does not reach the level which should be attainable, considering the level of technological development. The gap thus created becomes even larger due to the fact that markets are increasingly internationalized. We stretch the truth only a little if we say that nearly all markets are world markets. Enterprises offer increasing competition in international markets, characterized by continuous financial and technical innovation. If they are not sufficiently focused on export, new technical developments in the international arena may not be noted. Thus the gap between actual and potential growth in Europe can be ascribed, at least in part, to the bottlenecks in respect of the diffusion of application of new products and new production methods and to the lack of sensitivity to the internationalization of markets.

The view that technical change is ultimately the outcome of human activities, preferences and decisions implies that it can be influenced by economic and social policy. The frontiers have definitely shifted now that it is more widely understood that technical change is not a datum external to economics but endogenous to the economic process and therefore part of economic policy. Although history provides an ever-changing picture of technical change with a pattern of anything but equilibrium and a course of events characterized by 'technologically induced traverses, disequilibrium transitions between successive growth paths' (Abramowitz and David, 1973; see also Rosenberg, 1975) or by technological paradigms à la Dosi (Dosi, 1984), yet there is no plurality without unity, no interruption without continuity. Technical change is not so heterogeneous and chaotic that its present bears no relation to its past. The dynamics of economic life consist of the fact that to a certain extent the same scenarios recur.

Such paradoxes are not alien to the field of technical change. When rapid technical change is expected, the expectation itself will slow down the application of new techniques. In a rapidly changing world people tend to adopt a wait-and-see policy, which might in fact be desirable both from the private and from the public point of view (Rosenberg, 1976a and b).

The traditional role of economics is to explain the qualitative and quantitative increase in the satisfaction of human needs and to study the best ways of handling scarce resources. This implies that there is a central place in economics for the micro-economic analysis of technical and financial innovation. It may still surprise us that Keynes never paid any attention to technical change, but he did say that its absence causes secular stagnation (Keynes, 1936). Nowadays any fear of a deep and prolonged depression seems unfounded. The pool of technological knowledge is enormous; the possibilities are vast; by the end of this century households and enterprises will face an entirely different world, in particular because of information technology and telecommunication. However, we cannot conclude from this that – as Keynes optimistically stated – 'the economic problem may be solved' around the year 2030 (Keynes, 1931). It is more likely that the human mind will be faced with ever-growing problems of reconciling increasing needs and limited resources. It can be expected that environmental issues, in particular, will come to the fore.

New methods of forecasting technical change are being developed, and thought is being given to the economic effects of anticipating such change. Such efforts gain in importance as the process of technical change becomes less constrained by national frontiers. More and more markets are becoming world markets and are being internationalized. Hence, establishing criteria for economic policy involving technological change can no longer be done on only a national basis. Individual Western European countries must recognize that these economic processes are supranational in nature, and call for a concerted European policy.

It must be recognized that change involving technological development extends beyond the frontiers of economics. It embraces all aspects of human activity. With such recognition, and with broadly based social and scientific research, policies will be based on more solid ground than mere opinion, and crude dogmatism will be tempered by knowledge. Only in this way can technical and financial innovation be managed and controlled so that it will be the servant of human progress and not its master.

REFERENCES

Abramowitz, M. and David, P.A. (1973) Reinterpreting economic growth: parables and realities. *American Economic Review*, 429.

Dosi, G. (1984) *Technical Change and Industrial Transformation*, p. 16, Macmillan, London.

Keynes, J.M. (1931) *Essays in Persuasion*, p. 366, Macmillan, London.

Keynes, J.M. (1936) *The General Theory of Employment, Interest and Money*, pp. 217–21, Macmillan, London.

Morishima, M. (1982) *Why has Japan 'Succeeded'?* Cambridge University Press, Cambridge.

Rosenberg, N. (1975) Problems in the economist's conceptualization of technological innovation. *History of Political Economy*, 456–81.

Rosenberg, N. (1976a) On technological expectations. *Economic Journal*, 523–35.

Rosenberg, N. (1976b) *Perspectives on Technology*, Cambridge University Press, London.

Soete, L. (1986) Technological innovation and long waves: an inquiry into the nature and wealth of Christopher Freeman's thinking. In R. Macleod (ed.), *Technology and the Human Prospect*, p. 230, Frances Pinter, London.

Teece, D.J. (1986) Capturing value from technological innovations: integration, strategic patterning and licensing decisions. Working Papers Series in International Business, University of California, Berkeley Business School, Berkeley.

2

Industrial Structure and Technical Change

Giovanni Dosi and Luigi Orsenigo

This chapter concerns the relationship between industrial structure and technological innovation. Industrial structure can be described in terms of the size distribution of the firms in the industry, and also of the distribution of other characteristics, such as the firms' technological capabilities, organizational features and strategies. Technological innovation refers to changes in production processes and in the products manufactured by each firm.

The relationship between industrial structure and innovation runs both ways, and, in general, one may ask two types of question. First, one may investigate the influence of particular types of structure upon the rate and direction of technological change. Second, over time, structures change also as a result of the innovative strategies pursued by the various firms and the different levels of competitiveness so achieved. Thus, one may investigate the effect of different patterns of technical change on the evolution of industrial structures (Rosenberg, 1976 and 1982; Freeman, 1982; Nelson and Winter, 1982; Pavitt, 1984a).

In a biological analogy, the first level of investigation deals with the ways in which particular morphologies of individuals, species and ecosystems influence the generation of 'mutations', while the second analyses the selection processes and the ways in which mutations affect the genesis of new morphologies. The

The paper is partly based on the work of the authors with G. Silverberg on self-organization models of innovation diffusion and on research, in progress, by Dosi with D. Teece and S. Winter on the innovation boundaries of the firm. We thank B. Bianco for his help in the drafting of this paper.

coupled dynamics between these processes underlie industrial transformation. Of course, the evolution of industrial environments, unlike the biological analogy, also involves strategic behaviour by the agents with respect to the generation of their own 'mutations' (i.e. technological and organizational innovations) and learning in order to influence the environment to their own advantage.

Thus, structures influence what the agents can do and want to do in terms of innovative strategies, while the competitive process selects amongst different 'mutations' by giving an advantage to some firms by means of varying profitabilities and market shares, and penalizing others.

Understanding both the process of industrial transformation and the innovative performance of any industrial environment involves (1) some sort of taxonomic exercise on the characteristics of the 'structures' (e.g. large vs small firms, high concentration vs near-atomistic competition, highly skewed vs relatively even distributions of technological capabilities, etc.); (2) an analysis of the major characteristics of the innovative process; (3) the description of the processes through which the 'structures' influence the rate and direction of the generation of 'mutations', and, in the opposite direction, the ways in which innovations influence processes in firms of different sizes, organizational forms, etc.; (4) some sort of 'mapping' between stylized types of structures, innovation and competitive processes. Such an analysis, at one level, implies an understanding of the 'boundaries' of firms: e.g. to what degree can innovative and productive activities be efficiently internalized within a single firm? What is the relationship between the nature of a particular innovative process and the characteristics of a firm in terms of size, diversification, vertical integration and organizational features? At another level, it implies an understanding of the factors that affect *the allocation of resources to innovative efforts* and that may have to do with the nature of the various technologies, with the structural features of industries and firms, with the economic incentives that firms perceive and also with broader institutional factors such as the nature and rules of the financial system. Finally, it implies an understanding of *the processes of learning and selection* in each industry.

In the following section we will briefly discuss important features of technology and innovation and of industrial environments characterized by technical change. We will next consider the causal loop from industrial structures to technological innovation, discussing both the theory and some empirical evidence, and then deal with the opposite causal loop from the innovative process to changes in industrial structure. Finally, we will make some conjectures as to the role of financial institutions in so far as they affect the allocation of resources to innovation and the related industrial dynamics.

1   TECHNOLOGY, INNOVATION AND INDUSTRIAL STRUCTURE

Unlike the standard representation of technology as an information set concerning input combinations, we suggest that its description contains not only the list of productive inputs currently in use, but also components of hardly codifiable knowledge about the use of these inputs, often specific to the people and organizations which embody them, search and learning procedures about the improvement of production efficiency and the development of new products and methods of production.

Elsewhere, one of us has defined a 'technological paradigm' as the specific set of knowledge, associated with the exploitation of selected physical/chemical principles and the development of a given set of artifacts (Dosi, 1982 and 1984). Technological change involves a search, drawing on a variety of knowledge bases, ranging from publicly available scientific knowledge, to imitation of what other firms are doing, information coming from suppliers and customers and to the knowledge and capabilities developed within the firms themselves. Search procedures and knowledge bases are specific to each industry and to each technological paradigm. In some industries, for example, the search process is typically formalized in R & D laboratories; in others it is based on the engineering activities of design and development; in yet others it is mainly based on learning-by-doing and learning-by-using, often on the grounds of equipment-embodied innovations developed in other industries. Moreover, since the knowledge on which innovative activities are based is highly differentiated and specific to particular applications and particular organizations, firms are not likely to search by dipping into a freely available stock of 'information' but, instead, are likely to search 'locally' in areas which are proximate to their current production and research activities, and with degrees of success which are often conditional on their pre-existing capabilities. In other words, innovative activities involve varying levels of cumulativeness.

For any given innovative effort, the probability of successful innovative advances and the magnitude of these advances are related to the technological opportunities entailed in each technological paradigm. So, for example, new technological paradigms – often based on new scientific advances – such as microelectronics or biotechnology, present extremely wide opportunities for technological advance. Other – often 'older' – paradigms entail lower opportunities.

Moreover, technologies substantially differ in the degrees and forms in which they can be appropriated as profit-yielding assets. In other words, technologies embody varying mixtures of public-good aspects and privately appropriable features. This mixture and the mechanisms through which innovations are shielded from imitation differ from sector to sector. For example, in some cases, patents are fundamental means of appropriation; in others secrecy, lead-times, learning-curve effects, the costs and time required for duplication are more effective and important than patents. Superior sales and service structures and, more generally, the control of complementary assets are often essential to extract profits from technological innovations (Teece, 1986).

Finally, innovation presents an intrinsic uncertainty with regard to the technological and economic outcomes of search activities. Inevitably, they involve the creative production of new pieces of knowledge through the analysis of often ill-defined problems.

We suggest that the foregoing characterization of technology and innovation, in terms of different knowledge bases and different degrees of opportunity, secrecy, appropriability and uncertainty, also provides the basis for a taxonomic exercise on the innovative modes that one observes in different industries and also for the analysis of the determinants of the inter-sectoral and inter-firm differences in the rates of innovation. Specific

combinations of identifiable knowledge bases, sources of opportunity and appropriability conditions are termed a *technological
regime* (Winter, 1984; Nelson, 1986).

Let us now turn to the characteristics of industrial structures.
A first variable that can be used to describe an industry is the
absolute and relative size of the firms within that industry. It
happens that the average size of a firm varies significantly among
different industries. However, the size distribution of firms in
manufacturing in many cases resembles a Pareto distribution.
Industry-specific size distributions vary somewhat, but they rarely
diverge very much from log-normality. Irrespective of the precise
shape of the distribution, one tends to observe many small firms,
a few large firms and some very large firms. Clearly, in so far
as firms are multi-product enterprises and operate in different
industries, industrial structures, measured by firm-size, and market
structures, measured by market shares, are likely to differ, and
there are quite significant inter-industry variations in the degrees
of market concentration.

Incidentally, industrial economists have focused on these size
and concentration characteristics of industries and markets to the
point where they have neglected virtually all other factors.
However, we suggest that there are some other variables which
characterize industrial structures: firms within an industry differ
in more respects than just size and market share.

First, firms differ in terms of the level and distribution of their
accumulated technological capabilities. This is a consequence of
the partly secret and appropriable nature of technology mentioned
above. If technology were a free good, any firm would have
access to 'best-practice' process and product technologies. Instead,
firms are characterized by specific capabilities that often tend to
persist over time. In turn, these different capabilities, together
with different degrees of exploitation of static economies of scale
and different age distributions of the capital equipment, account
for the differences in unit cost across firms. Moreover, different
technological capabilities account for different performance
characteristics of firms' outputs. These differences between firms,
in terms of production efficiency and product performance, are
termed *technological asymmetries*. Thus, the degree of asymmetry
of an industrial structure measures the relative technological gap

between technologically 'worst-practice' and 'best-practice' firms and the asymmetry distribution represents the relative frequency of firms showing a certain production efficiency or price-weighted performance characteristic of output.[1]

Second, firms may differ in terms of their production technology and input combinations, even at roughly similar levels of efficiency, stemming from firm-specific histories of technological accumulation. An example of this is seen in the fact that there may be two, more or less equally efficient, oxygen- or electric-arc processes used in the production of steel, or two different patterns of automation of a certain mechanical output. Moreover, output characteristics may differ as a result of different combinations in the product–performance space (Metcalfe, 1985; Gibbons and Metcalfe, 1986), sometimes as a result of attempted product differentiation and market segmentation. These differences in production technologies and product characteristics which cannot be unequivocally ranked as 'better' or 'worse' are termed *technological varieties* of an industry.

Third, different firms, even when faced with identical innovative opportunities, and, more generally, identical environmental conditions, may well follow different strategies with regard to investments, allocation of resources to R & D, pricing, choice of innovative projects, scrapping decisions, diversification, target profitability and vertical integration. Moreover, in inter-industry comparisons or international comparisons within the same industry, one may find different patterns of interaction, such as price collusion vs competition and innovative aggressiveness vs prevalent imitative strategies.[2] Let us call these strategic differences *behaviour diversity*.

Finally, firms are likely to differ in terms of their organizational structure. Some may be vertically integrated and others may not; some are highly diversified, others are specialized. Moreover,

---

[1] Just to provide illustrative examples, think of (price-weighted) performance differences between, say, personal computers, or of the different fuel consumption, speed, acceleration and driving stability of different makes of car. For some attempts at measuring these output features along 'trajectories' of technological progress, see Gordon and Munson (1981), Dosi (1984) and Saviotti and Metcalfe (1984).

[2] Incidentally, note that this 'behavioural indeterminateness' emerges even if one were to believe that firms are neoclassical maximizers, wherever the equilibria are multiple and conditional on the agents' expectations about other agents' strategies.

firms differ in terms of their internal management structure. Let us call these aspects of industrial organization *organizational diversity*. To summarize, we describe industrial structure in terms of level and distribution of firm size, technological capabilities, technological variety, behavioural and organizational diversity.

2 FROM INDUSTRIAL STRUCTURE TO INNOVATIVE PERFORMANCE

The econometric evidence suggests an approximately log-linear relationship between firm size and innovative proxies. However, there is disagreement in the literature about whether the propensity to innovate shows 'increasing returns' with size. For example, Scherer (1965) argues in favour of a sort of inverted U-shaped relationship, with a relatively low share of innovation amongst small firms, increasing in the medium to large firms and then decreasing somewhat amongst the largest firms. Soete (1979) shows, on the contrary, 'increasing returns', or U-shaped relationships, for around one-third of his industry sample. Moreover, it can be reasonably argued that, if innovativeness is measured in terms of formal R & D expenditures or R & D employment, it underestimates the innovative contribution of small firms, for they sometimes develop innovations outside properly accounted R & D departments, while patenting measures underestimate the contribution of large firms because their propensity to patent seems to be lower than average; they often exploit their innovative advantages in other ways, such as secrecy, synergies between different research activities and brand loyalties. As regards the relationship between market concentration and innovation, one tends to find an inverted U-relationship, with a market structure intermediate between pure competition and monopoly as, seemingly, the most conducive to innovation (Kamien and Schwartz, 1982). In any case, in the latter studies, there exists a problem of identification, since the degree of concentration tends to be multicollinear with firm size.

However, in our view, the most serious problem is related to the underlying theoretical model. To what degree does the statistical evidence identify the 'true' effect of size and concentration on innovative activities and not, for example, a spurious correlation, with the correct causality running in the opposite direction? What are the effects on innovativeness of the other characteristics of industrial structure listed earlier?

The foregoing discussion of the characteristics of technology suggests that the size and concentration effects related to: economies of scale in R & D or, conversely, management inefficiencies in large organizations; indivisibilities in R & D projects or bureaucratic inertias and risk-aversions of large organizations; incentives from market power or lack of incentives from comfortable quasi-monopolistic positions; different degrees of self-financing and 'imperfections' on the capital markets, would be superimposed on the effect exerted by sector-specific conditions of opportunity and appropriability. In fact, even rough proxies for technological opportunities tend to explain a good deal of the inter-sectoral variance in the rates of innovation. Somewhat more refined empirical attempts to specify the opportunity and appropriability conditions of each industry, confirm their importance as explanatory variables of the propensity to innovate (Levin et al., 1985). The first attempt to 'map' relatively rich information on features of technological innovations with the characteristics of industries and firms was done in the UK by Pavitt (1984a).

Pavitt identifies four groups of industries, namely:

1 'Supplier-dominated' sectors. Innovations are mainly process innovations, embodied in capital equipment and intermediate inputs and originated by firms whose principle activity is outside these sectors. Supplier-dominated industries include textiles, clothing, leather, printing and publishing and wood products. In these sectors, the process of innovation is primarily a process of diffusion of best-practice capital goods and of innovative intermediate inputs, such as synthetic fibres, produced by other firms.

2 'Scale-intensive' sectors. Innovation concerns both processes and products, production activities generally involve mastering complex systems and, often, manufacturing complex products; economies of scale of various sorts are significant; firms tend to be large, they produce a relatively high

proportion of their own process technology, devote a relatively high proportion of their own resources to innovation, and tend to vertically integrate into the manufacturing of their own equipment. This group includes transport equipment, some electric consumer durables, metal manufacturing, food products, glass and cement.

3 'Specialized suppliers'. Innovative activities relate primarily to product innovations which enter other sectors as capital inputs. Firms tend to be relatively small, they operate in close contact with their users and embody a specialized knowledge in design and equipment-building. Typically, this group includes mechanical and instrument engineering.

4 'Science-based' sectors. Innovation is directly linked to technical paradigms made possible by scientific advances; opportunity is very high; innovative activities are formalized in R & D laboratories; a high proportion of their product innovation enters a wide number of sectors as capital or intermediate inputs; firms tend to be large. This group includes the electronics industry and most of the chemical industry.

This taxonomy is clearly consistent with the characteristics discussed above.

In 'supplier-dominated' industries one may expect the appropriability of innovation to be relatively low, while technological opportunities are mainly determined exogenously, in the sectors producing capital equipment and components. Thus, one may expect a firm's own informal learning processes, e.g. from production-based experience as well as industry-wide via 'epidemic' diffusion of information and skills, to assume a relatively high level of importance. Moreover, the evolution of technologies over time, their relative profitabilities, the minimum size thresholds which make innovation activities feasible and profitable, are shaped by the interaction between 'specialized suppliers' and 'supplier-dominated' industries. These user–producer interdependencies induce 'spill-over effects', which are in a sense analogous to epidemic learning. Clearly, whenever innovations are introduced by 'specialized suppliers' horizontal diffusion amongst users will be encouraged by the suppliers. Thus, transfers of knowledge between users and producers and the technical sophistication of the users (Lundvall, 1984) together with the development of 'network externalities' (David, 1985; Katz and Shapiro, 1983) will be very important in determining both technical change amongst users and amongst suppliers. In these cases, the process of innovation can be seen as a process of continuous learning associated with the development of informal institutions, untraded interdependences between suppliers and users, adaptation and cooperation.[3]

At the other extreme of Pavitt's taxonomy, consider science-based industries. Here, technological opportunities for innovating are generally very high and appropriability – stemming from cumulativeness of technical advances, lead-times and patents – is generally quite high. Moreover, the fundamental scientific knowledge base is exploited economically through formalized search efforts. Thus, one may expect technical change to rely relatively more on expensive search processes (R & D). The premium for innovative success is generally high: successful 'Schumpeterian' firms often become large rather quickly and cumulativeness of technical advances frequently allows them to remain large and successful thereafter.

Finally, 'scale-intensive' industries are likely to show varying combinations of the two opposite 'ideal types' of innovation and diffusion discussed above. Analogous to the 'supplier-dominated' model, various forms of learning related to the development and use of capital equipment are likely to be very imporant. However, unlike 'supplier-dominated' industries, technological synergies between production and use of groups of innovations are often internalized via horizontal and vertical integration or quasi-integration (Mowery, 1981; Teece, 1982); the development and adoption of new technologies are associated with the exploitation of static and dynamic economies of scale; formal search/learning through R & D is highly complementary to 'informal' learning and diffusion of technological knowledge.

Taxonomical exercises on technological regimes, forms of industrial organization and patterns of innovation such as the

---

[3] 'Network economies' and varying mixtures of cooperation and competition which characterize specialized industrial districts, such as those frequently found in several Italian areas, are good examples of these phenomena (Brusco, 1982).

one by Pavitt on opportunity and appropriability represent a fundamental aspect of the development of a theory of technical change and industrial structure, as they provide observation-based generalizations about basic 'types' of innovative activities and industrial environments, i.e. on basic 'morphologies'.

Theoretically complementary questions are, clearly: Why should these patterns be observed rather than others? What are the processes that yield particular configurations of technological regimes and industrial structures? How do the characteristics of both technologies and structures affect the dynamics of innovative performances and structures? Under what conditions do certain structures remain relatively stable over time? What is the interaction between innovation and structural dynamics?

In brief, the question concerns the relationship between observed morphologies and dynamic processes and it is central in evolutionary/self-organization theories of economic change.

Unfortunately, formal developments of this approach are relatively recent and empirical research is still lagging behind these developments. We shall review some findings obtained from sector case studies and model simulations, and suggest some, more speculative, conjectures.

3   PATTERNS OF INNOVATION AND INDUSTRIAL DYNAMICS

Let us start by considering some properties of evolutionary environments characterized by technical change.

First, note that evolutionary environments with technical change present 'disequilibrium' dynamics: 'better' and 'worse' firms coexist and there might well be a 'redundance' of technological solutions present in the market. There is always uncertainty regarding the technical and market outcomes of each firm's innovative efforts, what the other competitors will do and what will happen in the future; firms interact strategically at different levels. Innovation is a fundamental competitive weapon which allows relatively successful firms to increase their profitability and market shares. Under these circumstances the dynamics of an industry can be represented as the process of self-organization whereby technology, structures and behaviour interact to produce relatively ordered evolutionary paths for any single industry or for the economy as a whole, while, in turn, the evolving morphology of the system feeds back on the capabilities, incentives, constraints and behaviours of individual agents (Dosi et al., 1986; Dosi and Orsenigo, 1987).

Second, evolution is, in general, driven by two processes, namely learning and innovation, and competition and selection. As we shall see, the different modes and balances between the two processes are part of the categorization of different evolutionary processes.

Third, again in general terms, evolutionary processes can generate a wide variety of dynamic paths, subject to various kinds of non-linearities. Small events, different initial conditions, out-of-equilibrium behaviour and micro-fluctuations may heavily influence the evolutionary paths and the asymptotic states of the system. That is, evolutionary processes are generally path-dependent and behaviour-dependent (Allen, 1987; Arthur, 1987).

Thus, the understanding of how and why certain types of state emerge requires a rich specification of initial conditions, of the nature of learning processes and patterns of interactions between the economic agents.

Let us now discuss some empirical and theoretical propositions about the relationship between the nature of the processes and the nature of the states, beginning with a quite straightforward property of evolutionary environments, namely what market structures are endogenous to the industrial dynamics. The dynamics of size and market share of an individual firm are crucially influenced by that firm's relative innovative/imitative success and, as a consequence, this also affects the dynamics of market concentration. Thus, over time, one observes two interrelated processes. One is the dynamics of innovation as a function of firm size. The other is the dynamics of size as a function of innovation. It follows that whenever innovativeness is approximately size-unbiased, the dominant process runs from innovative capabilities to market structures, and not the other way round. For example, suppose that changes in 'innovativeness' (u), however measured, are a random variable with respect to size and that the 'competitiveness' of the i-firm E (i) is linear in its innovativeness.

At time t

$$E(i,t) = \lambda \; u(i,t). \tag{2.1}$$

Following Silverberg (1987), the rate of change of the market share of the i-firm $f(i)$ at time t, is

$$f(i,t) = A \; [E(i,t) - \bar{E} \; (t)] \; f(i), \quad A>0 \tag{2.1}$$

where the dot stands for the rates of change and $E(t)$ is the 'average' competitiveness of the industry, weighted by market shares.

That is,

$$f(i,t) = A\lambda[u(i,t) - \Sigma \; (i) \; u \; (i,t) \; f(i,t)] \; f(i), \tag{2.2}$$

which corresponds to a sort of 'Gibrat law' interpreted in terms of the innovation-based competitiveness of each firm. With size-unbiasedness of innovative changes, the evolutionary dynamics of market structure depend on the 'sensitivity' of market shares (λ) for differential innovative capabilities and for the mean and distribution of 'realized' innovations [$u(i,t)$], which in turn depend on the technology-related opportunities to innovate and the appropriability regime affecting the incentive to commit resources to the innovative search.

In fact, model simulations and industry studies show the importance of technological regimes for the evolution of industrial structures and, in particular, the importance of innovation and fast imitation for firms' growth. Sectoral case studies were carried out by Philips (1971) on aircraft, Dosi (1984) and Malerba (1985) on semiconductors, Orsenigo (1987) on biotechnology, Momigliano (1985) on data processing, Pavitt (1986) on chips and Altschuler et al. (1984) on automobiles. On simulation models, see Nelson and Winter (1982); Iwai (1984a and b); Winter (1984); Dosi et al. (1986); Eliasson (1986).

Plausibly, high levels of technological opportunity and high degrees of private appropriability of the economic benefits from innovation tend to be associated with high rates of innovation, relatively large firm size and relatively high degrees of industrial concentration. A relatively high probability of, and premium for, innovative success yields a relatively fast growth of innovating firms.

Strong degrees of cumulativeness of technical advance strengthen this tendency, allowing early innovators to grow and remain large and successful thereafter. On the contrary, low degrees of appropriability and ease of imitation are a countervailing force preventing the attainment of a high degree of concentration; similarly, a strong exercise of market power by leading firms tends to limit concentration, in that it is associated with the search for high profit margins and therefore non-aggressive pricing and investment policies. Moreover, the nature of the knowledge base underpinning innovative search has important consequences for the pattern of industrial dynamics. Whenever the knowledge on which a firm draws when searching for innovations is relatively simple, generic and accessible to a multitude of firms and individuals, new entrants do not find strong entry barriers.

On the other hand, whenever the relevant knowledge base is highly cumulative, 'local', and firm-specific, large incumbent firms are in a better position to exploit technological opportunities and strengthen their innovative lead, cumulatively building upon their technological capabilities (Winter, 1984).

On similar grounds it has been argued (Abernathy and Utterback, 1975; Gort and Klepper, 1982; Dosi, 1984) that in the early stages of the development of a new technological paradigm, when the relevant knowledge base is still generic and precise technological trajectories have not yet emerged and settled, market structure is likely to be rather fluid, with high rates of natality and mortality of new 'Schumpeterian' firms which exploit temporary oligopolistic positions linked to specific innovations. Later on – as technological trajectories become more precisely defined and technical knowledge becomes increasingly specific and internalized within the boundaries of particular firms – innovation becomes increasingly cumulative and a relatively more stable oligopolistic structure is likely to emerge.

Finally, it has been argued (Pavitt, 1984a; Nelson, 1986) that the characteristics of technology, in terms of opportunity, appropriability conditions and the nature of the knowledge base, can also explain the localization of innovative activities in large or small firms and across different sectors. As mentioned above, companies will tend to internalize their innovative activities when technological opportunities are high and/or whenever there are economies of scale and scope in R & D or production, or when upstream or downstream firms can become dangerous competitors if they obtain access to the relevant knowhow. Conversely, reliance on external suppliers or users of technology is likely to be more frequent when the relevant knowledge base is relatively simple and generic, when innovative activities do not require high R & D expenditures and formalized learning processes, but offer room for specialization in specific niches, or when technological capabilities are high and diffused across a large number of firms. In brief, both sectoral studies and simulation models appear to show the fundamental importance of the characteristics of technologies in terms of the evolution of industrial structures.

However, given these broad technology-specific characteristics, the initial structural conditions of industries and the institutional context where innovative activities take place matter as well. In particular, we conjecture, they affect the observed inter-regional and inter-national differences in industrial structure and innovative performance within the same industry or the same technology.

First, given the cumulative nature of the process of innovation, the level and the distribution of technological capabilities within the industry contribute to determine the number and the characteristics of the firms that are actually ready and able to exploit any given set of technological opportunities.

Second, the existing pattern of technological asymmetries represents a sort of 'factor of order' which limits the set of feasible strategies available to each firm and tends to order them hierarchically. In other words, the degree and distribution of technological asymmetries are likely to perform as a first approximation predictor of short-term performance, having a role analogous to those entry/mobility barriers upon which the 'structuralist' tradition in industrial economies has focused (Bain, 1956; Downie, 1958; Sylos-Labini, 1967; Caves and Porter, 1977 and 1978).

Third, it is clear that the higher the average technological capabilities of potential innovators of the new technologies, the faster their rates of innovation, since high technological capabilities also mean the ability to search efficiently, to evaluate the properties of the innovations, to imitate and/or use them quickly, to possibly improve them, to exchange information with suppliers and to interact with them.

These capabilities, however, are generally unevenly distributed between different firms, and their distributions are at least as important as their averages.

Thus, in the fourth place, holding the characteristics of different technologies constant, one may advance the hypothesis that the more skewed the distribution of capabilities and the higher its standard deviation, the more important is the role of 'selection', compared to learning, as an engine of technical change. In other words, the capability gap between different firms will tend to introduce high differences in competitiveness and produce high market shares for the leaders and the 'killing off' of the laggard firms. Empirically, one finds an impressionistic corroboration of this hypothesis by comparing the industrial structures in high-technology sectors of countries in the vanguard and those following: concentration is often much higher in the latter. For the case of semiconductors, this has been illustrated by Dosi (1984).

A corollary of this hypothesis is that whenever average capabilities are low, a higher rate of innovation may be achieved through higher levels of asymmetry and relatively more hierarchical industrial organizations. This hypothesis mirrors somewhat Stiglitz' discussion of choices between 'bad' and 'good' projects under 'polyarchy' vs 'hierarchy' (Sah and Stiglitz, 1986).

Conversely, low levels of asymmetry imply that a relatively large number of firms will compete using the new technology, imitation will be comparatively easy and various forms of learning will prevent markets from establishing a harsh selection discipline. Moreover, the initial distribution of market shares of firms having different technological capabilities influences the speed and patterns of innovation.

In the fifth place, imagine different competing technologies. Here, diversity based on technological variety is fundamental: in a sense, the evolutionary dynamics of the industry are sustained by its 'redundancy of genetic forms' (Eliasson, 1986; Gibbons and Metcalfe, 1986; Metcalfe, 1987).

More generally, if technological capabilities are relatively evenly distributed and there are several innovative directions, the probability of 'accepting' an innovation will depend on variety, i.e. on the existence of many different groups of firms, differentiated in their knowledge bases, criteria of technical choice and search procedures. The other side of the coin is that with too great a variety learning processes for each technology might be rather slow: one may even conceive of a limiting case where no technology becomes profitable enough to be a success.

The sixth point is that behavioural diversity affects both the rate of diffusion and the relative importance of selection and learning mechanisms. Technological and market expectations clearly affect the rate of adoption of new technologies (David and Olsen, 1984; Dosi et al., 1986; Silverberg, 1987). Moreover, the 'market aggressiveness' of the most capable companies, those that innovate earlier and/or have lower costs of production, determine the rates of survival and the market shares of the relatively backward firms and thus the strictness of market selection of the 'fittest'. If market selection is highly efficient, that is, if all innovative advantages are transformed immediately into greater competitiveness and larger market share, diffusion will take place quite rapidly. However, note that highly efficient market selection might actually hamper the take-off and diffusion of new technologies whenever the latter are not initially very profitable: unsuccessful experiments are punished severely and fast, so that potentially promising technologies might not be given enough time to develop and to be improved. More generally, this brief taxonomic exercise highlights some of the factors which affect the different combinations possible between two different types of innovation, based on selection, variety and 'creative destruction' on the one hand and on 'creative and cumulative accumulation' of technological knowledge on the other, within each firm and in the industrial environment as a whole (Pavitt, 1986). The change over time of the mixture of these two types of innovation and of the variation across industries has a technological and a behavioural dimension. The more cumulative learning occurs, for any set of characteristics of each technological paradigm, the more industrial evolution is likely to rely on 'centralized' processes of organization of production and innovative development.

Finally, the behaviour of agents and the specific nature of the selection and learning mechanisms are constrained by the institutional set-up of the environment. Social rules, inherited norms and attitudes, the laws of organization of the linkages between and within various groups of economic agents do matter in determining the set of admissible strategies and behaviours, and also of observed innovative performances. The specification of the institutional rules constraining individual behaviour becomes therefore a crucial task in the analysis of the patterns of technical change, which accounts for the observed differences across countries within the same technologies.

4 EVOLUTION, RESOURCE ALLOCATION AND INNOVATIVE PERFORMANCE

The picture of the co-evolution of technologies and industrial structures is 'Schumpeterian' in the sense that there is tension between the efficiency in the allocation of resources and the incentives to innovate; between what afterwards prove to be the 'best' technological trajectories and the trial-and-error processes driving technological search; between 'incremental' improvements along existing technological trajectories and the exploration of new ones; between strengthening the existing industrial structure and making the challenges of new entrants easier; between the 'carrot' of innovation-related benefits and the 'stick' of competition (Nelson, 1981 and 1986).

The competitive process, in general, provides a positive feedback mechanism whereby relatively successful agents enjoy above-average availability of financial resources. The availability of capital would not be affected by history, if financial markets were 'perfect' in a neoclassical sense. However, even the neoclassical tradition recognizes the role of 'imperfections' and 'information asymmetries' in the financing of innovative search and in dynamic environments in general (Leland and Pyle, 1977; Stiglitz, 1982; Arrow, 1983; Diamond, 1984; Bernanke and Gertler, 1985; Fama, 1985). In other words, history does matter and the institutional framework for finance and project selection matters too, in terms of innovative performance (Sah and Stiglitz, 1986; Pelikan, 1987). History and institutions do matter in our approach, which stresses the path-dependency and behaviour-dependency of evolutionary structures and related performances.

What can be said, in general, about the relationship between the nature of the financial system, industrial dynamics and allocation of resources to innovation?

Recall the empirical dichotomy between 'market-oriented' and 'institution-oriented' financial systems (Rybczynsky, 1974; Zysman, 1983), with the former being predominantly based on 'impersonal' exchanges of ownership rights and contingency claims and the latter on more 'institutional' relationships of ownership and/or control and/or exchanges of special information between providers and users of financial resources. As an example of the former, one may cite the contemporary UK and US, and of the latter several continental European countries and Japan. The contemporary debate about the effects of these institutions on technological dynamisms, and, more generally, economic performance, seems somewhat contradictory: for instance, in the UK and US it is often alleged that a short-time view of capital markets tends to induce industrial firms to place a disproportionate emphasis on quarterly stock exchange performance, and less on long-term commitment to technological innovation and growth.[4] Conversely, in Europe and in Japan, the behaviour of financial institutions is said to be so conservative and bureaucratic as to penalize in particular new 'Schumpeterian' ventures.

It seems plausible that, just as a talent for allocating resources to particularly innovative projects is something that is built up cumulatively so also is an aptitude on the part of investors to allocate resources to particular firms (Pelikan, 1987). Thus, specialized institutions are likely to 'choose' more competently, to develop specialized knowledge, to foster relatively more 'learning' than selection and to favour the development and reproduction of relatively stable and concentrated industrial structures. On the other hand, 'knowledge' goes along with an 'exclusion effect': knowing certain things and having certain 'visions' often makes it harder to see 'other things'. There may be a trade-off between the depth and the scope of information (Williamson, 1975; Dosi and Egidi, 1987). Thus, one would expect to observe a trade-off between the efficiency of industry-

---

[4] See, for instance, Carrington and Edwards (1979), Lorenz (1979) and Crotty (1985).

linked financial institutions such as investment banks in allocating resources along relatively established technological trajectories and their ability to back highly uncertain 'experiments' on new technological paradigms (see also Ergas, 1986).

We suggest that market-oriented systems do apply more to countries that happen to be on or near the 'technological frontier'. Under these circumstances, variety, exploration and trial-and-error search are likely to be very important elements of technological progress. The development of a venture-capital market is an institution that matches these processes. Conversely, formal bank–industry relationships are more likely, also on historical grounds, in follower countries that often require relatively long-term commitments of resources to accumulate technological competence, often despite absolute and comparative disadvantages and unfavourable profitability, especially in the newest/most promising technological paradigms.

Now, consider the role of 'financial discipline', expressed by certain debt/equity ratios, or returns-on-equity, or some other target. In general, a relatively harsh 'discipline' toughens the selection mechanisms, thus decreasing both technological asymmetries and variety. In doing so, it improves the allocative efficiency of resources, since it decreases the standard deviation between 'best' and 'worst' firms, but, in non-stationary environments it may also decrease the scope for explorations, seemingly 'deviant' behaviours and longer-term strategies. Putting it somewhat more conventionally, it may 'optimize' faster in the neighbourhood of what could be a local optimum, albeit decreasing the chances – in a path-dependent world – of reaching future, possibly superior, 'hills'. Moreover, it may well slow down the growth of the most successful firms (Schuette, 1980; Nelson and Winter, 1982; Eliasson, 1986).

REFERENCES

Abernathy, W.G. and Utterback, J.M. (1975) A dynamic model of product and process innovation. *Omega*, 639–56.

Allen, P. (1987) Evolution, innovation and economics. Paper prepared for the IFIAS Workshop on 'Technical Change and Economic Theory: The Global Process of Development', Maastricht.

Altschuler, A., Anderson, M., Jones, D.T. and Womack, J. (1984) *The Future of the Automobile*. Allen & Unwin, London.

Arrow, K.J. (1983) Innovation in large and small firms. In J. Ronen (ed.), *Entrepreneurship*. Lexington Books, Lexington, Mass.

Arthur, W.B. (1987) Competing technologies: an overview. Paper prepared for the IFIAS Workshop on 'Technical Change and Economic Theory: The Global Process of Development', Maastricht.

Bain, J.S. (1956) *Barriers to New Competition*. Harvard University Press, Cambridge, Mass.

Bernanke, B. and Gertler, M. (1985) Banking in general equilibrium. NBER Working Paper no. 1647. Cambridge, Mass.

Brusco, S. (1982) The Emilian model: productive decentralisation and social integration. *Cambridge Journal of Economics*, 167–85.

Carrington, J.C. and Edwards, G.T. (1979) *Financing Industrial Development*. Macmillan, London.

Caves, R.E. and Porter, M.E. (1977) From entry barriers to mobility barriers: conjectural decisions and contrived deterrence to new competition. *Quarterly Journal of Economics*, 241–62.

Caves, R.E. and Porter, M.E. (1978) Market structure, oligopoly and stability of market shares. *Journal of Industrial Economics*, 289–313.

Crotty, J. (1985) Real and financial sector interaction in macromodels: reflections on monocausal theories of investment instability. Paper presented at the Conference 'The Impact of Technology, Labour Markets and Financial Structures on Economic Progress and Stability', Washington University, St Louis.

David, P. (1985) Cliometrics and the economics of qwerty. *American Economic Review*, 332–8.

David, P. and Olsen, T.E. (1984) *Anticipated Automation. A Rational Expectations Model of Technology Diffusion*. Stanford University Press, Stanford, Cal.

Diamond, D. (1984) Financial intermediation and delegated monitoring. *Review of Economic Studies*, 393–415.

Dosi, G. (1982) Technological paradigms and technological trajectories. A suggested interpretation of the determinants and directions of technical change. *Research Policy*, 147–62.

Dosi, G. (1984) *Technical Change and Industrial Transformation*. Macmillan, London.

Dosi, G. and Egidi, M. (1987) Substantive and procedural uncertainty. An exploration of economic behaviours in complex and changing environments. Paper presented at the Conference 'Flexible Automation and New Work Modes', Paris, DRC Discussion Papers, SPRU, University of Sussex.

Dosi, G. and Orsenigo, L. (1987) Structures, performances and change in evolutionary environments. Paper prepared for the IFIAS Workshop 'Technical Change and Economic Theory: The Global Process of Development', Maastricht.

Dosi, G., Orsenigo, L. and Silverberg, G. (1986) Innovation, diversity and diffusion. A self-organization model. Paper presented at the Conference on 'Innovation Diffusion', Venice, SPRU, University of Sussex.

Downie, J. (1958) The Competitive Process. Duckworth, London.

Eliasson, G. (1986) *The Firm and Financial Markets in the Swedish Micro-to-Macro Model*. IUI, Stockholm.

Ergas, H. (1986) *Does Technology Policy Matter?* OECD, Paris.

Fama, E.F. (1985) What's different about banks? *Journal of Monetary Economics*, 29–39.

Freeman, C. (1982) *The Economics of Industrial Innovation*. Frances Pinter, London.

Gibbons, M. and Metcalfe, J.S. (1986) Technological variety and the process of competition. Paper presented at the Conference on 'Innovation Diffusion', Venice, SPRU, University of Sussex.

Gordon, T.S. and Munson, T.R. (1981) *Research into Technology Output Measures*. The Future Group, Glastonbury, Conn.

Gort, M. and Klepper, S. (1982) Time paths in the diffusion of product innovations. *Economic Journal*, 630–54.

Iwai, K. (1984a) Schumpeterian dynamics. Part I: An evolutionary model of innovation and imitation. *Journal of Economic Behaviour and Organization*, 159–90.

Iwai, K. (1984b) Schumpeterian dynamics. Part II: Technological progress, firm growth and economic selection. *Journal of Economic Behaviour and Organization*, 321–51.

Kamien, M. and Schwartz, N. (1982) *Market Structure and Innovation*. Cambridge University Press, Cambridge.

Katz, M.L. and Shapiro, C. (1983) Network externalities, competition and compatibility. Woodrow Wilson School, Discussion Papers in Economics no. 54, Princeton University, Princeton, N.J.

Leland, H.E. and Pyle, D.H. (1977), Informational asymmetries, financial structure and financial intermediation. *Journal of Finance*, 371–87.

Levin, R., Cohen, W.M. and Mowery, D.C. (1985) RD appropriability, opportunity, and market structure: new evidence on some Schumpeterian hypotheses. *American Economic Review*, 20–5.

Lorenz, C. (1979) *Investing in Success: how to profit from design and innovation*. Anglo-American Foundation for the Study of Industrial Society.

Lundvall, B.A. (1984) User/producer interaction and innovation. Paper presented at the TIP Workshop, Aalborg.

Malerba, F. (1985) *The Semi-Conductor Business*. Frances Pinter, London.

Metcalfe, J.S. (1985) *On Technological Competition*. University of Manchester.

Metcalfe, J.S. (1987) Diffusion of innovations. Paper presented at the IFIAS Workshop on 'Technical Change and Economic Theory: The Global Process of Development', Maastricht.

Momigliano, F. (1985) Le tecnologie dell'informazione: effetti economici e politiche pubbliche. In A. Ruberti (ed.), *Tecnologia Domani*. Laterza-Seat, Bari.

Mowery, D.C. (1981) *The Nature of the Firm and the Organization of Research: an investigation of the relationship between contract and in-house research*. Harvard University Press, Cambridge, Mass.

Nelson, R.R. (1981) Research on productivity growth and productivity differences: dead ends and new departures. *Journal of Economic Literature*, 1029–65.

Nelson, R.R. (1986) *Institutional supporting of technical change in industry*. Paper presented at the IFIAS Workshop on 'Technical Change and Economic Theory: The Global Process of Development', Maastricht.

Nelson, R.R. and Winter, S. (1982) *An Evolutionary Theory of Economic Change*. Belknap Press (Harvard University Press), Cambridge, Mass.

Orsenigo, L. (1987) Institutions, markets and governments in the development of a new technological paradigm: the case of biotechnology in Italy and an international comparison. Paper presented at the ECPR Workshop on 'Politics and Technologies', Amsterdam.

Pavitt, K. (1984a) Sectoral patterns of technical change: towards a taxonomy and a theory. *Research Policy*, 343–73.

Pavitt, K. (1984b) *International Patterns of Technological Accumulation*. SPRU, University of Sussex, Brighton.

Pavitt, K. (1986) Chips and 'trajectories': how does the semiconductor influence the sources and directions of technical change? In R.M. Macleod (ed.), *Technology and the Human Prospect*. Frances Pinter, London.

Pavitt, K., Robson, M. and Townsend, J. (1986) The size distribution of innovating firms in the UK: 1945–1983. Paper presented at the Conference on 'Innovation Diffusion', Venice, SPRU, University of Sussex.

Pelikan, P. (1987) Can the innovation system of capitalism be outperformed? Paper presented at the IFIAS Workshop on 'Technical

Change and Economic Theory: The Global Process of Development', Maastricht.

Philips, A. (1971) *Technology and Market Structure: a study of the aircraft industry*. D.C. Heath, Lexington, Mass.

Rybczynsky, R.M. (1974) Business finance in the EEC, USA and Japan. *Three Banks Review*, 58–72.

Rosenberg, N. (1976), *Perspectives on Technology*. Cambridge University Press, Cambridge.

Rosenberg, N. (1982) *Inside the Black Box*. Cambridge University Press, Cambridge.

Sah, R.K. and Stiglitz, J.E. (1986) The architecture of economic systems: hierarchies and polyarchies. *American Economic Review*, 716–28.

Saviotti, P. and Metcalfe, J.S. (1984) A theoretical approach to the construction of technology output indicators. *Research Policy*, 141–9.

Scherer, F.M. (1965) Firm size, market structure, opportunity, and the output of patented inventions. *American Economic Review*, 1097–126.

Schuette, H. (1980) The role of firm financial rules and a simple capital market in an evolutionary model. Ph.D. Dissertation, University of Michigan, Ann Arbor.

Silverberg, G. (1987) Modelling economic dynamics and technical change: mathematical approaches to self-organization and evolution. Paper presented at the IFIAS Workshop on 'Technical Change and Economic Theory: The Global Process of Development', Maastricht.

Soete, L. (1979) Firm size and inventive activity: the evidence reconsidered. *European Economic Review*, 312–90.

Stiglitz, J.E. (1982) Information and capital markets in financial economics. In W. Sharpe and C. Lootner (eds), *Essays in Honor of Paul Lootner*. Prentice-Hall, Englewood Cliffs, N.J.

Sylos-Labini, P. (1967) *Oligopoly and Technical Progress*. 2nd edn, Harvard University Press, Cambridge, Mass.

Teece, D. (1982) Toward an economic theory of the multi-products firm. *Journal of Economic Behaviour and Organization*, 39–63.

Teece, D. (1986) Profiting from technological innovation. *Research Policy*, 285–305.

Williamson, O. (1975) *Markets and Hierarchies: analysis and antitrust implications*. Free Press, New York.

Winter, S. (1984) Schumpeterian competition in alternative technological regimes. *Journal of Economic Behaviour and Organization*, 287–320.

Zysman, J. (1983) *Governments, Markets and Growth. Financial systems and the politics of industrial change*. Cornell University Press, Ithaca, N.Y.

3

Diffusion: The Spread of New Technology to Firms, Sectors, and Nations

Chris Freeman

We owe to Schumpeter (1939) the distinction between invention, innovation and diffusion of innovations, which has since been generally adopted in most research on technical change. Inventions are identifiable contributions to technological change which are frequently, but by no means always, the subject of patent applications. However, many inventions (and patents) remain unused and do not affect the economic system. They become economically significant only when embodied in innovations. The process of innovation is the first introduction of new products, techniques and systems into the economy. Successful innovations lead to a process of diffusion across firms and countries. It is diffusion which leads to perceptible and widespread effects on the growth of productivity and of the economy generally.

But although analytically valuable, like all such distinctions, this classification obscures some important aspects of the relationship between the three categories. As Rosenberg (1975, 1982) in particular, has forcefully pointed out, many improvement inventions and innovations take place *during* the process of diffusion itself, both as a result of user experience and as a result of competition between suppliers. It is quite obvious, for example, that the word-processors or robots which are being widely diffused today are not the same products as their forerunners ten years ago.

I am grateful to Carlotta Perez for permission to develop this chapter on the basis of an earlier joint paper for the Venice Conference on Innovation Diffusion in March 1986.

The point is an extremely important one and, as we shall see, it has had a considerable influence on the approach adopted to diffusion research in the 1960s and the 1980s respectively. Much of the empirical and theoretical work of the 1960s was based on models that implicitly or explicitly assumed an unchanging product (or process) diffusing through an unchanging environment to a determinate unchanging number of potential adopters. Moreover, it was assumed that the diffusion of one product was unaffected by the parallel diffusion of other products and processes.

Whilst such assumptions are defensible in terms of simplification, they are clearly unrealistic in the case of many product and process innovations. One of the main concerns of this chapter is with the interrelationships between clusters of new products and processes, i.e. with the diffusion of 'new technological systems', and 'techno-economic paradigms' combining many interrelated innovations.

After a brief introduction we start by considering the simplified 'standard' or 'fundamental' model of diffusion generally adopted by sociologists and economists in the 1950s and 1960s. Following discussion of some of the limitations of this model, we then discuss the concepts of new technology systems and of techno-economic paradigms. The concept of change of techno-economic paradigm is then applied to the case of information and communication technology (ICT) in the 1980s and specifically to the diffusion of this new paradigm across a variety of manufacturing and service sectors. Finally, we extend this discussion to the case of the international diffusion of new technologies and the specific problems of the European Economic Community.

1 INTRODUCTION

The importance of diffusion is accepted by all schools of economic thought but it is only recently that it has become the subject of more systematic research and analysis. As late as 1972 Rosenberg commented that it was a 'striking historiographical fact that the serious study of the diffusion of new techniques is an activity no more than fifteen years old ... Even today, if we focus upon the most critical events of the industrial revolution ... our ignorance of the rate at which new techniques were adopted, and the factors accounting for these rates is, if not total, certainly no cause for professional self-congratulation' (quoted in McArthur, 1987). The lack of attention to *diffusion*, by comparison with invention and innovation had some consequences not just for historians and for economic theory but for the type of technology policy pursued in most countries in the post-war period.

It is a commonplace that the competitive strength of a country, a branch of industry or a firm is related to its capacity to adopt and exploit new technology efficiently in its products and processes. However, the inventions and innovations which are taken up by thousands of enterprises all over the world will not usually be made by those enterprises themselves. Indeed, the vast majority will originate elsewhere and consequently it is quite possible for a country (or a firm) to make rapid technical progress without contributing very much, or even anything at all, to original research or development. Most of the technical change which is taking place in the world is the result of the dissemination of knowledge and the diffusion of innovations, within and between countries, universities and firms.

This does not mean of course that the original ('first in the world') research and innovation is unimportant. On the contrary, it is clearly the fountainhead of all the subsequent diffusion and applications. Without the original research on nuclear physics and on macro-molecular chemistry the modern electronics and plastics industries would scarcely exist anywhere and there would certainly be no nuclear reactors. Obviously, without the first commercial introduction of a new product or process (innovation) there cannot be any subsequent diffusion, improvement or learning process. In this sense original fundamental research and radical technical innovation are crucial for the world economy as a whole. Without them, technical progress would ultimately dry up, even though economic growth could continue for a long time on the basis of the dissemination of the existing stock of knowledge and 'best practice'.

Moreover, even the import and assimilation of new knowledge and innovations from firms elsewhere often requires some involvement in research and development to attain the necessary depth of undertanding and capability. Nevertheless, it is probably true that science and technology policies since the Second World War have concentrated too much on the R & D system and not enough on diffusion. Even the largest super-powers cannot hope to be self-sufficient in science and technology or indeed to make more than a fraction of all the important technical innovations. Moreover, within the economies of the super-powers (and other countries) the overall rate of technical change will depend not just on the leading firms, but even more on the speed and efficiency with which new technology diffuses to the whole of the potential adopter population. As will be argued in Section 7 below, the adoption of some Japanese organizational and technical innovations is now likely to be especially important for Europe.

The critical importance of diffusion came out in a major study of the diffusion of process innovations made by a number of European research institutes, including the IFO in the German Federal Republic, the IUI in Sweden and the NIESR in the UK (Ray, 1984). The study showed that the UK was frequently the first, or among the first, of eight countries to introduce a process innovation, but often the last to diffuse it through the potential adopter populations. Swedish and German firms on the other hand, although not the first innovators, were usually the quickest to diffuse innovations through industries. They also achieved more efficient exploitation of the new processes during the diffusion process. Such studies have much to teach us about labour and capital productivity differences across countries and industries, since it is the average performance of many firms which determines such broad trends.

Consequently, Paul David (1986) was right to point out that diffusion has been relatively neglected in post-war policies for science, technology and industry:

> Innovation has thus become our cherished child, doted upon by all concerned with maintaining competitiveness and renewing failing industries; whereas diffusion has fallen into the woeful role of Cinderella, a drudge-like creature who tends to be overlooked when the summons arrives to attend the Technology Policy Ball. As a case in point, consider that in the Report of the President's Commission on Industrial

Competitiveness (1985) the words 'diffusion' and 'adoption' do not appear anywhere in the summary of recommendations dealing with the nation's technological resources.

Similar comments could be made about many reports on science and technology policy in Europe. On both theoretical and practical grounds, therefore, there is ample justification for concentrating attention on diffusion and attempting to gain a better understanding of the diffusion process both at national and international levels. To some extent this has already occurred. The Venice DAEST Conference on Innovation Diffusion (March 1986) was remarkable both in terms of the participation by the international economics profession, as well as other social scientists, and in terms of the stimulus it gave to diffusion research. It was a landmark in the study of technical change in much the same way as the National Bureau of Economic Research Conference stimulated the study of invention and innovation in the 1960s (NBER, 1962). The three-volume report of the Venice conference (Arcangeli et al., 1988, forthcoming) will become a major reference point for future research on diffusion.

2 THE 'FUNDAMENTAL' OR 'STANDARD' MODEL OF DIFFUSION

In his paper at the Venice Conference Rogers (1986) drew attention to the explosion of diffusion research in the 1960s and 1970s. By contrast, when he made his pioneering survey of diffusion research twenty-five years earlier (Rogers, 1962), he could find only one example of industrial diffusion research by an economist in the 1950s – the study by Bruce Williams of the tunnel oven in the pottery industry. The earlier research by Griliches (1957) related to the diffusion of agricultural innovations, and the sociologists and geographers who dominated diffusion research in the 1950s concentrated largely on agricultural, medical and educational innovations.

This stream of empirical research found that the typical pattern of diffusion followed an S-shaped curve of the type shown in figure 3.1 and sought to explain this typical pattern in terms of

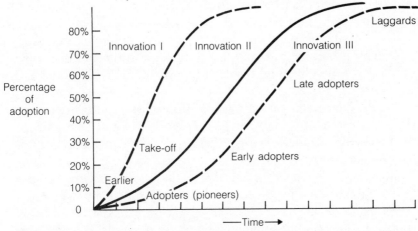

Figure 3.1 Diffusion is the process by which (1) an innovation (2) is communicated through certain channels (3) over time (4) among the members of a social system.
Source: Adapted from Rogers (1986)

communication channels and various characteristics of the potential adopter population, such as age, education, travel, attitudes to risk and so forth. This led to the familiar classification of adopters as 'pioneers', 'early adopters', 'late adopters' and 'laggards'.

These early studies in the 1950s were strongly influenced by models used in epidemiology. They frequently represented the commonly observed patterns of diffusion, as in 'epidemic' studies, by a logistic curve, with a slow and hesitant early start, followed by a rapid exponential increase and a final phase of slow asymptotic approach to a ceiling level. The 'epidemic' model recognized that as an infection spreads, the number of individuals who may transmit the disease increases, accelerating the rate of diffusion towards an upper limit governed by the size of the population at risk. As this limit is approached, diffusion necessarily slows down. Sociologists tended to ascribe the supposed prevalence of this pattern to the combination of information dissemination with the social characteristics of various groups of the adopter population: the small number of pioneering, risk-taking inno-vators, the larger numbers of those who adopted only after convincing demonstration effects or advice from 'opinion leaders' and the tail of rather conservative (and in some accounts, older) laggards. The 'pioneers' corresponded to the first 'infected' individuals in the epidemic model; as their numbers increased, information became available to much larger numbers of people until only a few 'healthy' resistant or isolated individuals did not succumb.

As we have seen, at this stage economists contributed very little to this stream of research, despite its obvious relevance to the theory of technical change, the theory of the firm and cyclical phenomena in the economy.

This picture changed drastically in the 1960s, mainly because of the great impetus given to diffusion studies by Mansfield (1961) and Griliches (1957) in the US. Mansfield not only contributed a number of empirical studies of diffusion in various industries and services including steel, brewing, railways and mining (figure 3.2), but also developed an explanatory theory and model, which was very influential in much subsequent research in the 1960s and 1970s. Indeed, it is quite often described

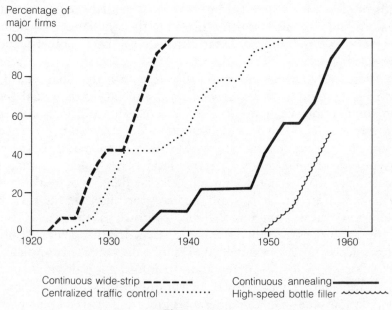

Figure 3.2
Source: Mansfield (1961)

as the 'standard' model. Mansfield sought to explain the observed patterns of diffusion in terms of rational decision-making by potential adopters, taking into account (1) profitability, (2) scale of investment and (3) a learning process, based on communications between prior adopters and potential adopters. According to Mansfield's (1961) studies, the pattern of diffusion in the industries that he studied could be explained mainly in terms of these three variables. Unlike some other researchers in the field of agricultural innovation he found that age of key decision-makers did not apparently influence the outcome. Size of firm, however, was a significant factor in relation to those innovations involving a high threshold of investment (point (2) above). Relative factor-saving advantages were not a major concern, provided the profitability criterion was satisfied.

In a very useful discussion of models used in diffusion research since the Second World War, Mahajan and Peterson (1985) treat Mansfield's model as one of a family developed in the 1950s and 1960s, many of which were strongly influenced by assumptions and modelling techniques used in epidemiological research.

The 'fundamental' model used by these researchers was of the form expressed by the differential equation:

$$\frac{dN(t)}{dt} = g(t)[\overline{N} - N(t)]$$

with the boundary conditions

$$N(t = t_0) = N_0$$

where

$N(t)$ = cumulative number of adopters at time t;
$\overline{N}$ = total number of potential adopters in the social system at time t;

$\dfrac{dN(t)}{dt}$ = rate of diffusion at time t;

$g(t)$ = the coefficient of diffusion;
N_0 = the cumulative number of adopters at time t_0.

Mahajan and Peterson (1985) divide these types of 'fundamental model' into three categories: 'external influence', 'internal influence' and 'mixed influence'. In the first category the coefficient of diffusion $g(t)$ is defined as an index of external influence, usually representing the influence of change agents on the diffusion process. In the second category, characteristic of most economic work on diffusion in the 1960s, including Mansfield's own model, the rate of diffusion is treated solely 'as a function of inter-personal communication or social interaction between prior adopters and potential adopters in the social system', i.e. it is a pure imitation diffusion model, in which the communication of adopter information and attitudes is the fundamental factor.

Although some diffusion situations do correspond approximately to the assumptions of either the 'internal influence' or the 'external influence' model, the great majority do not. In most cases both 'external' and 'internal' influences affect the diffusion process. Consequently, a third category of 'mixed influence' models was soon developed incorporating assumptions of both the other categories. These were used initially to forecast sales of consumer durables (e.g. Bass, 1969).

Mahajan and Peterson (1985) describe various attempts to overcome the limitations of the 'fundamental' model with respect to two mathematical properties: the point of inflection and symmetry. They point out that:

> In practice, as well as in theory, the maximum rate of diffusion of an innovation (the 'point of inflection') should be able to occur at any time during the diffusion process. Additionally, diffusion patterns can be expected to be non-symmetric as well as symmetric. However, both the internal-influence and the mixed-influence models at best offer only limited flexibility in terms of these two properties.

However, the improved models that they report (e.g. Floyd, 1968; Sharif and Kabir, 1976), although more flexible than the 'fundamental' model, do not overcome the most important weaknesses in that stage of diffusion research, which are discussed in the following section. In an interesting comment they also point out that Von Bertelanffy's (1957) model was surprisingly neglected, although it already offered solutions to some of the mathematical difficulties of the 'fundamental' model.

3 CRITIQUE OF THE 'STANDARD' MODEL AND THE 'FUNDAMENTAL' MODEL IN THE 1970S AND 1980s

During the 1960s and 1970s many empirical studies, both in Europe and the US, were inspired by the early work of Mansfield. These studies generally confirmed the importance of those factors which he identified, but they also pointed to some difficulties associated with this model of diffusion, and to the variety of circumstances attending different types of innovation, different sectors of the economy and different national economic and social environments.

Among the difficulties pointed out by various researchers (e.g. Bradbury et al., 1972; Stoneman, 1976; Gold, 1981) were those attending *ex ante* calculations of potential profitability, the *systems* aspects of many decisions to innovate and the 'non-economic' aspects of adoption (managerial attitudes, industrial relations, etc.). A number of researchers questioned the 'rationality' assumption in Mansfield's model because of imperfect information and apparently 'irrational' behaviour by some potential adopters. Metcalfe (1970) found in his study of the Lancashire cotton industry that a large tail of potential adopters did not actually adopt at all, even where clear-cut economic and technical advantages from the use of a size-box had been amply demonstrated and the pay-back period was less than a year. The importance of capital saving cost advantages was stressed in some studies, especially in relation to the investment behaviour of smaller firms, but in this case the obvious advantages apparently had little effect.

More recently, in the late 1970s and 1980s, some more fundamental issues have been raised. As we have seen, a number of researchers have pointed out that the early diffusion models, although very useful for many purposes, neglected changes in the environment during the process of diffusion and changes in the innovation itself during that process. In the twenty years since the development of Mansfield's original model, a good deal of empirical work on diffusion of innovations has provided a much better basis for generalization. Several authors, such as Stoneman

(1976), Davies (1979) and Arcangeli (1985), have especially stressed the importance of the *supply* side, and Mansfield himself has also emphasized this (1977). This concern had already found some expression in the 1960s with the development of the 'mixed influence' models.

In a seminal paper, Metcalfe (1981) stressed the role of profitability for suppliers (as opposed to adopters), and the influence of secondary innovations affecting profitability both for suppliers and adopters:

> Gold (1981) and Davies (1979) ... have argued that observed diffusion paths primarily reflect changes in the innovation and adoption environment rather than a process of learning within a static situation. As Gold observes, the standard diffusion model rests on the implicit static assumption that the diffusion levels reached in later years also represent active adoption prospects during earlier years.

This criticism is clearly fundamental in areas such as computer technology. When computers were first used, even very well-informed businessmen, such as T. J. Watson Senior, then head of IBM, took the view that diffusion would be limited to a handful of customers, such as the Bureau of the Census and the Defense Department. They did not foresee a population of potential adopters in the business sector at large. Even in the 1950s, when rapid diffusion of computers was taking place for business applications, it was generally thought that their diffusion would be restricted to large firms, because of their relatively high investment costs. When mini-computers became available in the 1960s the effects of the micro-processor in enlarging enormously the potential adopter population was seldom foreseen. Even when the micro-processor arrived it was some time before it was recognized that this population now included all households as well as all firms.

This is an obvious case where, as Stoneman (1976) pointed out, any satisfactory diffusion theory would have to take into account price and quality changes during the diffusion process, as well as skill availability and the traditional factors used in the standard diffusion model. The problem can be only partially overcome by treating the successive generations of electronic computers as distinct products because, among many other reasons, the adoption prospects for each new generation are strongly affected by the installed capacity of previous generations and the related software.

Mahajan and Peterson (1985) summarize the limitations of the whole family of 'fundamental' diffusion models under seven headings. They point out that many of the (not wholly realistic) simplifying assumptions used in this type of model were originally adopted to facilitate analytical solutions, rather than to reflect accurately the empirically observed phenomena.

For example, one assumption is that the diffusion process is 'binary' (Sharif and Ramanathan, 1982): the innovation is regarded as a discrete event and is either adopted or not. As a result the models do not take into account the complexity of the awareness, decision-making, evaluation and testing process within firms. Moreover, each innovation is assumed to be independent of others and multiple adoptions (repeat purchases) are excluded from consideration. The size and the geographical boundaries of the potential adopter population are assumed to be finite and fixed and are not allowed to grow during the course of the diffusion process, in response to changes in technical characteristics or price, or as a result of changes in the external environment. In the 'internal influence' models it is assumed that the effects of interaction between prior and potential adopters are the same regardless of time of interaction and adoption, i.e. the coefficient of internal influences is assumed to be constant over time.

They suggest that these limitations of the static standard diffusion model can be partly overcome by developing new models which relax some of the more questionable assumptions. For example, in their own work (1979) they have developed dynamic models which take into account some aspects of the interdependence of innovations (complementarity and substitution effects) and of multi-stage decision-making. They also report other work (e.g. Dodson and Muller, 1978; Horsky and Simon, 1983) which attempts to incorporate such factors as the influence of price changes, profitability, advertising and other promotion behaviour by change agents.

Increasingly, the active role of suppliers is recognized as a key factor, as for example in the work of Issidoridis (1986) on the diffusion of new machinery in the Greek textile industry. Sections 4–7 of this chapter concentrate on the systems aspect of diffusion, rather than discrete innovations, and on the supply side interacting with demand.

4 SCHUMPETER'S 'CREATIVE GALES OF DESTRUCTION', NEW TECHNOLOGY SYSTEMS AND CHANGES OF TECHNO-ECONOMIC PARADIGM

Metcalfe (1981, 1987) has developed a comprehensive model of diffusion combining both supply-side profitability and adopter profitability.

As he has pointed out, recent work on diffusion has important points of connection with the earlier work of Kuznets, Burns and Schumpeter, which related the diffusion of major technical innovations to changes in the structure of industry and cyclical patterns of development in the economy as a whole. Whereas many empirical studies in the 1960s and 1970s concentrated on the diffusion of individual products, there is now a growing recognition of the interdependence of clusters of technical and organizational–managerial innovations and of the role of the institutional and social framework within which diffusion proceeds.

This section is concerned with these 'meta-diffusion' studies and seeks to clarify the concepts of 'new technology systems' (Freeman et al., 1982), 'techno-economic paradigms' (Perez, 1983, 1985), 'technological paradigms' (Dosi, 1982), 'technological regimes' and 'natural trajectories' of technology (Nelson and Winter, 1977).

The emphasis of this Schumpeterian approach is not so much on the individual new product or new process, or on technological improvements to the existing array of products and services, as on entirely new technologies. Diffusion research on individual products or processes is, of course, relevant to analysis and forecasting of specific innovations within the broad spectrum of new technologies. But if we are considering clusters of related innovations with the potential to affect a very broad range of products and processes and even the economy as a whole, then the Schumpeterian type of approach would seem more relevant. The concern here is with the complementarities and externalities of families of interrelated technical and social innovations. In Schumpeter's analysis, these successive technological revolutions underlie the 'Kondratiev' cycles, or long waves of economic development.

In this type of approach an important first step is the identification of the characteristics of those major changes in technology that have such widespread consequences that they merit some such description as 'technological revolution', or 'change in techno-economic paradigm', or 'change in technological regime'. Any such taxonomy or classification system must, of course, do some violence to the infinite complexity of the real processes of technical and economic change. Nevertheless, a taxonomy is essential both for analytical purposes and as a tool for empirical research (Freeman, 1984; Freeman and Perez, 1986). It is useful to distinguish between four categories of innovations and their diffusion: incremental innovations, radical innovations, new technology systems and changes of techno-economic paradigm.

Incremental innovations occur more or less continuously, although at differing rates in different industries, but they are concerned only with improvements in the existing array of products and processes of production. They are reflected in the official measures of economic growth by changes in the coefficients in the existing input–output matrix. Although their combined effect is extremely important in the growth of productivity, no single one has dramatic effects. Examples include the improvements described by Hollander (1965) in his study of DuPont rayon plants.

Radical innovations are discontinuous events and they have been the main concern of most diffusion studies, frequently showing the typical sigmoid pattern identified in the standard diffusion models and in product cycle theory. Logically, they lead to the inclusion of new rows and columns in the matrix of input–output tables, but in practice such changes occur only with long time-lags, as in the case of computers.

New technological systems are 'constellations' (Keirstead, 1948) of innovations which are technically and economically interrelated. Obvious examples are the clusters of synthetic materials innovations, petrochemical innovations and plastics machinery innovations introduced in the 1930s, 1940s and 1950s. Another example is the 'cluster' of electrically driven household consumer durables innovations. Nelson and Winter's 'natural trajectories' help to explain the technical interrelatedness of these clusters of radical and incremental innovations, but economic interdependencies are also important, as for example in the habituation to consumer credit systems in the purchase of consumer durables, or the externalities in skills which become available as a technology matures.

Changes of techno-economic paradigm correspond to the 'creative gales of destruction' which are at the heart of Schumpeter's long-wave theory. The introduction of electric power or steam power are examples of such fundamental transformations. A change of this kind carries with it many clusters of radical and incremental innovations, and may embody a number of new technology systems. A vital characteristic of this fourth type of technical change is that it has pervasive effects throughout the economy, i.e. it not only leads to the emergence of a new range of products, services, systems and industries in its own right, it also affects, directly or indirectly, almost every other branch of the economy. The expression 'techno-economic' rather than 'technological paradigm' emphasizes that the changes involved go beyond specific product or process technologies and affect the input cost structure and conditions of production and distribution throughout the system. This fourth category would correspond to Nelson and Winter's concept of 'general natural trajectories' and, once established as the dominant influence on engineers, designers and managers, becomes a 'technological regime' for several decades. In this perspective Schumpeter's long cycles may be seen as a succession of techno-economic paradigms.

We now turn to an elaboration of the main characteristics of techno-economic paradigms and their patterns of diffusion through long waves of economic development. A new techno-economic paradigm develops initially within the old, showing its decisive advantages during the 'downswing' phase of the previous

Kondratiev cycle. However, it becomes established as a dominant technological regime only after a crisis of structural adjustment, involving fundamental social and institutional changes, as well as the replacement of the leading motive branches of the economy.

5 THE DIFFUSION OF THE NEW INFORMATION AND COMMUNICATION TECHNOLOGY PARADIGM

As made clear in Section 4 above, the concept of techno-economic paradigm developed by Perez (1983, 1985) is much wider than 'clusters' of innovations or even of 'technology systems'. We are referring to a combination of interrelated product and process, technical, organizational and managerial innovations, permitting a quantum jump in potential productivity for all or most of the economy and opening up an unusually wide range of *new* investment and profit opportunities. Such a new techno-economic paradigm implies a unique new combination of decisive technical, economic and social advantages, and becomes the dominant technological style for an entire phase of economic growth and development.

Clearly, one major characteristic of the diffusion pattern of a new techno-economic paradigm is its spread from the initial industries or areas of application to a much wider range of industries and services and the economy as a whole. A 'paradigm' change is a radical transformation of the prevailing engineering and managerial common sense for best productivity and most profitable practice, which is applicable to almost any industry. Section 6 discusses the way in which the information technology paradigm is diffusing very unevenly across various sectors of the economy. Section 7 discusses international aspects of diffusion. Here we discuss the main characteristics of a techno-economic paradigm.

The organizing principle of each successive paradigm and the justification for the expression techno-economic paradigm is to be found not only in a new range of products and systems, but in the dynamics of the relative *cost* structure of all possible inputs to production. Perez (1983) argues that in each new paradigm, a particular input or set of inputs, which may be described as the 'key factor' of that paradigm, fulfils the following conditions:

1 Clearly perceived low and rapidly falling relative cost. As Rosenberg (1975) and other economists have pointed out, small changes in the relative input cost structure have little or no effect on the behaviour of engineers, designers and researchers. Only major and persistent changes have the power to transform the decision rules and 'common sense' procedures for engineers and managers (Perez, 1985; Freeman and Soete, 1987).

2 Apparently almost unlimited availability of supply over long periods. Temporary shortages may of course occur in a period of rapid build-up in demand for the new key factor, but the prospect must be clear that there are no major barriers to an enormous long-term increase in supply. This is an essential condition for the confidence to take major investment decisions that depend on this long-term availability.

3 Clear potential for the use or incorporation of the new key factor or factors in many products and processes throughout the economic system; either directly or (more commonly) through a set of related innovations, which both reduce the cost and change the quality of capital equipment, labour inputs and other inputs to the system.

This combination of characteristics holds today for microelectronics and telecommunications. It held until recently for oil, which underlay the post-war boom (the fourth Kondratiev upswing). Before that, and more tentatively, the role of key factor was played by low-cost steel in the *belle epoque* before the First World War (the third Kondratiev upswing) and by low-cost coal and steam-powered transport in the 'Victorian' boom of the nineteenth century.

Clearly, every one of these inputs identified as a 'key factor' in each period existed (and was in use) long before the new paradigm developed. However, its full potential was only recognized when the previous key factor and its related constellation of technologies gave indications of approaching limits to the potential for further increasing productivity or for new profitable investment.

From a purely technical point of view, the explosive surge of interrelated innovations involved in a technological revolution, could probably have occurred earlier. But there are strong economic factors that first of all delay but later stimulate diffusion and improvement innovations. The massive externalities created to favour the diffusion and generalization of an existing paradigm act as a powerful deterrent to change for a prolonged period. The availability of skills, capital equipment, components, markets and enabling institutions is an extremely powerful combination favouring the already established techno-economic paradigm. It is only when productivity along the old trajectories shows persistent limits to growth and future profits are seriously threatened that the high risks and costs of the new technologies appear as clearly justified. The frustrations and difficulties involved in the early diffusion of computer-related innovations were often described in the 1950s and 1960s.

As a new techno-economic paradigm takes shape, the new key factor appears not as an isolated input, but rather at the core of a rapidly growing system of technical, social and managerial innovations, some related to the production of the key factor itself and others to its utilization. At first these innovations may appear (and may be in fact pursued) as a means for overcoming the specific bottlenecks of the old technologies, but the new key factor soon acquires its own dynamics and successive innovations take place through an intensive (and interactive) feedback process, spurred by the limits to growth which are increasingly apparent under the old paradigm.

Clearly, this approach implies a framework for diffusion research which stresses the systems context rather than the individual product. Clearly, too, it differs radically from the dominant conceptualization of changing factor costs in neoclassical economic theory, although it has points of contact, such as the persistent search for least-cost combinations of factor inputs. Most formulations of neoclassical theory put the main emphasis on varying combinations of labour and capital and on substitution between them, and implicitly or explicitly assume responsiveness even to small changes in these relative factor prices in either direction. Our approach stresses the system's response to *major* changes in the price of *new* inputs, and *new* technologies which exploit their potential to reduce costs of both labour and capital, as a result of new total factor input combinations and organizational–managerial innovations. Once the new technology is widely adopted, the change is generally irreversible. Brian Arthur's (1985, 1986) work on path dependence shows very clearly why this is so.

It is a clear implication of this way of conceptualizing successive techno-economic paradigms that a new paradigm emerges in a world still dominated by an old paradigm and begins to demonstrate its comparative advantages at first only in one or a few sectors. There is no possibility of a new paradigm displacing an old one until it has first clearly demonstrated such advantages and until the supply of the new key factor or factors already satisfies the three conditions described above: falling costs, rapidly increasing supply and pervasive applications. Thus, a period of rapid growth in the supply of the key factor(s) occurs already *before* the new paradigm is established as the dominant one, and continues when it is the prevailing regime. This was clearly evident in the growth of the semiconductor industry, integrated circuits and very large-scale integration (VLSI) from the 1950s to the 1980s.

The technological regime, which predominated in the post-war boom of the 1950s and 1960s, was based on low-cost oil and energy-intensive materials (especially petrochemicals and synthetics), and was led by giant oil, chemical, automobile and other mass durable goods producers. Its 'ideal' type of productive organization at the plant level was the continuous flow assembly line turning out massive quantities of identical units. The paradigm required a vast infrastructural network of motorways, roads, traffic control, service stations, oil and petrol distribution systems, which was promoted by public investment on a large scale already in the 1930s, but more massively in the post-war period. Both civil and military expenditures of governments played a very important part in stimulating aggregate demand, as well as social innovations in consumer credit systems.

Today, with cheap microelectronics widely available, with prices expected to fall still further and with related new developments in computers and telecommunications, it is no longer 'common sense' to continue along the (now expensive) path of energy- and material-intensive inflexible mass production.

The new 'ideal' information-intensive productive organization now emerging increasingly links design, management, production and marketing into one integrated system – a process which may be described as 'systemation' and goes far beyond the earlier concepts of mechanization and automation. Firms organized on this new basis, whether in the computer industry, such as IBM, or in the clothing industry, such as Benetton, can produce a flexible and rapidly changing mix of products and services. Growth tends increasingly to be led by the electronics and information sectors, taking advantage of the growing externalities provided by an all-encompassing telecommunications infrastructure, which will ultimately bring down to extremely low levels the costs of transmitting very large quantities of information all over the world.

The skill profile associated with the new techno-economic paradigm appears to change from the concentration on middle-range craft and supervisory skills, characteristic of the 'Fordist' mass production paradigm, to increasingly high- and low-range qualifications and from narrow specialization to broader multi-purpose basic skills for information handling. Diversity and flexibility at all levels substitute for homogeneity and dedicated systems.

The transformation of the profile of capital equipment is no less radical. Computers are increasingly associated with all types of productive equipment, as in CNC machine tools, robotics and process control instruments, as well as with the design process through CAD, and with administrative functions through data-processing systems, all linked by data transmission equipment. According to some estimates, computer-based capital equipment already accounts for nearly half of all new fixed investment in plant and equipment in the US.

A special supplement to the *Economist* (30 May 1987) entitled 'Factory of the Future' outlined the complete reorganization of the production system that is now taking place and is far more important than any particular discrete piece of equipment, even though the associated investment may take place incrementally and involve much trial and error.

For the first time in three-quarters of a century the factory is being reinvented from scratch. Long, narrow production lines with men crawling all over them – a feature of manufacturing everywhere since the early days of the car-making dynasties – are being ripped apart and replaced with clusters of all-purpose machines huddled in cells run by computers and served by nimble-fingered robots. The whole shape of the industrial landscape is changing in the process. The name of the game in manufacturing has become not simply quality or low cost but 'flexibility' – the quest to give the customer his or her own personalized design, but with the cheapness and availability of mass-produced items. Savile Row at High Street prices. In short nothing less than a whole new style of manufacturing is in the process of being defined.

It is because of this 'new style of manufacturing' that diffusion research can no longer concentrate, as in the 1960s, on discrete products but must take full account of system changes as well. For this reason there is now a proliferation of studies on the diffusion of 'computer-integrated manufacturing', 'flexible manufacturing systems', 'computer-aided design' and so forth (see, for example, Arcangeli et al., 1987).

But changes in the services industries are no less profound than in manufacturing. For the first time many service industries, such as banking and insurance are now promoting rapid technical change accompanied by a high level of investment in computer-based equipment.

The deep structural problems involved in this change of paradigm are now evident in all parts of the world. Among the manifestations are the acute and persistent shortage of the high-level skills associated with the new paradigm, even in countries with high levels of general unemployment, and the persistent surplus capacity in the older 'smokestack', energy-intensive industries, such as steel, oil refining and petrochemicals.

As a result there is a growing search for new social and political solutions in such areas as flexible working time, shorter working hours, re-education and retraining systems, regional policies based on creating conditions for information technology (rather than tax incentives to capital-intensive mass production industries), new financial systems, possible decentralization of management and government, and access to data banks and information networks at all levels. If the Keynesian revolution and the profound transformation of social institutions in the Second World War and its aftermath were required to unleash the fourth Kondratiev upswing, then social innovations on a much more significant scale are likely to be needed now. This applies especially to the international dimension of world economic development.

6 CROSS-SECTOR DIFFUSION AND DIFFERENTIAL GROWTH RATES OF PRODUCTIVITY

In describing the advantages of a new techno-economic paradigm, we have repeatedly stressed the ability to bring about a major increase in productivity. However, the *actual* rates of productivity increase have declined since the 1960s in most industrial countries. How is this apparent paradox to be explained?

First, it is essential to keep in mind that the new paradigm has been diffusing in a world still dominated by the older, energy-intensive mass production paradigm. The symptoms of diminishing returns to the massive investment in this old paradigm have been especially evident in declining capital productivity in most industrial sectors in almost all OECD countries since the late 1960s. But they have also become apparent in the declining rate of increase in labour productivity.

Second, in assessing the growing impact of the new techno-economic paradigm, it is necessary to take into account the problems of structural adjustment, before a 'good match' is achieved between the new paradigm and the institutional framework. This process is very uneven between different countries and different industrial sectors. Therefore, in examining these phenomena it is absolutely essential to move to a disaggregated level of analysis, since what we are discussing is the extremely uneven diffusion of a new paradigm from a few leading sectors to the economy as a whole.

When we analyse changes in labour productivity and in capital productivity over the past twenty years at a sufficiently disaggregated level, then we find the following picture:

1 The sectors with the highest rates of growth in labour productivity are the electronic industries, and especially the computer industry and the electronic component industry. These are the industries which make the greatest use of their own technology for design, production, stock control, marketing and management. They are also the only industrial sectors that show a substantial rise in *capital* productivity. They are the sectors that demonstrated the advantages of the new technologies for everyone else and may be described as the 'carrier' and 'motive' branches of the new paradigm.

2 In those sectors which have been heavily penetrated by microelectronics, both in their product and process technology, there is also evidence of a considerable rise in labour productivity and even some advance in capital productivity in the most recent period. This applies, for example, to the scientific instruments industry, to the telecommunications industry and to the watch industry. These sectors have now virtually become a part of the electronics industry.

3 In sectors where microelectronics has been used on an increasing scale over the past ten years, but older technologies still predominate in product and process technology, there is a very uneven picture. Some firms have achieved very high productivity increases, some have stagnated, whilst others actually show a decline in productivity. This is the case, for example, in the printing industry, in the machine-building industries and in the clothing industry. This uneven picture is completely consistent with Salter's (1966) vision of the spread of new technologies within established industries through new capital investment. In many cases information technology is introduced in a piece-meal fashion in one department or for one activity and not as part of an integrated system. For example, one or a few CNC machine tools are introduced, or a few robots or word-processors. These are small 'islands' of automation. This is not yet computer-integrated manufacturing or office systems and does not yet

achieve anything approaching the full *potential* productivity gains. There may even be a temporary fall in productivity, because of the lack of the necessary skills in design, in software, in production engineering, in maintenance and in management generally. Problems of institutional and social adaptation are extremely important, and flexibility in this social response is very varied between countries, as well as between enterprises. Among European countries, Germany, Italy and Sweden appear to have been particularly successful in making progress in the area of 'mechatronics', but the US, which has been quite successful in achieving productivity gains in the microelectronics area (although less so than Japan), has been rather unsuccessful in the mechatronics area, with the partial exception of defence-based industries.

4 Sectors producing standardized homogeneous commodities on a flow production basis in large plants have made considerable use of information technology in their process control systems and in various management applications. They were indeed among the earliest users of computers for these purposes. This applies for example to the petrochemical, oil, steel and cement industries. This has helped them to achieve considerable improvements in their use of energy and materials, but the gains in labour productivity have often been less than in the 1950s and 1960s, whilst capital productivity usually shows a marked decline. To understand this phenomenon it is essential to recognize that these industries are amongst those most heavily affected by the shift from an energy-intensive and materials-intensive mass production technological paradigm to an information-intensive paradigm. At the height of the consumer durables and vehicles consumption boom of the 1950s and 1960s, they were achieving strong labour productivity gains based on big plant economies of scale. But with the change in technological paradigm, the slowdown in the world economy and the rise in energy prices in the 1970s, they now often face problems of surplus capacity and high unit costs based on below-capacity production levels.

5 Service sectors which are completely based on information technology – software services, data banks, computerized information services, design services, etc., are among the fastest

growing and (for individual firms), the most profitable activities in the leading industrial countries. But although their growth potential is enormous they so far account for only a small proportion of total service output and employment. Productivity statistics are extremely difficult to generate, but inferential evidence suggests high rates of growth.

6   Some other service sectors have been considerably affected by information technology, such as banking, insurance and distribution. In these sectors, although the diffusion of new technology is extremely uneven, both by firm and by country, there is evidence of significant gains in labour productivity. This phenomenon is rather important because hitherto it has often been observed that the service sector of the economy was not capable of achieving the type of labour productivity gains achieved in manufacturing. Information technology now offers the potential (and in some cases already the reality) of achieving such gains outside manufacturing. However, the progress of technology depends heavily on institutional and structural changes and skill availabilities.

7   In most service sectors, information technology still has diffused only to a small extent, and these areas are still characterized by very low labour productivity gains, or none at all. The stagnation in labour productivity in these sectors may be attributed to the *lack* of information technology, but it certainly cannot be attributed to the impact of information technology. These account for by far the larger part of the tertiary sector.

8   Finally, in many industrialized economies there are sectors which have shown labour productivity gains over the past ten years, which are due far more to structural rationalization than to the direct impact of new technology. Examples are in the textile and food industries and also some of those sectors discussed in item 4 above, where plant closures and rationalization have been implemented. Since in any industry there is always a 'tail' of low productivity plants, a significant rise in *average* labour productivity can always be achieved simply as a result of scrapping

the older generations of plant, even without any further technical improvements in the more recent plants, which can now work closer to full capacity. This may be described as the 'Verdun' effect in contrast to the 'Verdoorn' effect of the high boom period.

Summing up this discussion, it is not difficult to see that the slowdown in average labour productivity gains over the 1970s and 1980s, which has been a worldwide phenomenon by comparison with the 1950s and 1960s, is precisely the aggregate outcome of a structural crisis of adaptation or change of techno-economic paradigm, which has accentuated the uneven development in different sectors of the economy.

On the one hand, the previously dominant energy-intensive mass production paradigm or 'technological regime' was reaching limits of productivity and profitability gains, due to a combination of exhaustion of economies of scale, erosion of profit margins through 'swarming', market saturation in some sectors, diminishing returns to technical activities (Wolf's Law) and cost pressures on input prices. On the other hand, the new paradigm, which offers the possibility of renewal of productivity gains and increased profitability, has so far deeply affected only a few leading-edge industries and services.

The full realization of the productivity gains that can be achieved as a result of information technology depends on the diffusion of the new paradigm throughout the economy. This in turn will be possible only as a result of many social and institutional changes, which will involve interrelated organizational and technical innovations, as well as a large increase in new skills and a transformation of the existing capital stock.

7 CONCLUSIONS: THE INTERNATIONAL DIFFUSION OF A NEW TECHNO-ECONOMIC PARADIGM

In this chapter I have tentatively suggested that the concept of changes in techno-economic paradigm may offer an explanatory framework, within which the study of the diffusion of discrete product and process innovations may more fruitfully proceed. In such an approach emphasis would be placed on the institutional factors affecting the behaviour of both users and suppliers of innovations and on the enabling role of policies which might accelerate or retard diffusion. Comparative international studies of the type pioneered by Nabseth and Ray could be particularly important in this approach (Ray, 1984).

It is in this context that comparisons between the EEC countries, the US, Japan and other European countries are of outstanding interest. There are, of course, enormous problems of definition and measurement but what most of these studies seem to show is that Japan is ahead of both the US and the EEC in the rapid adoption of new ICT systems, especially in the 'mechatronics' area of manufacturing (Freeman, 1987).

The very rapid Japanese diffusion of robotics, CNC machine tools and, more generally, of flexible manufacturing systems may be attributed primarily to a combination of institutional factors and policies promoting both cross-sector diffusion and intra-firm diffusion of the new techno-economic paradigm.

The distinctive feature of a techno-economic paradigm is that it has effects in every sector of the economy, providing scope everywhere for renewal of productivity increases through a combination of organizational, social and technical innovations and for a broad range of new and improved products and services. As we have seen in section 6, the main problem in periods of change of paradigm is not so much in the leading-edge industries (in this case computers and VLSI) as in the adaptation of the rest of the economy. It is here that the type of structural and institutional inertia problems identified by Perez are acute, and that national policies and new regulatory regimes are especially important.

The Japanese economy has been particularly successful in adapting the new paradigm to the needs of some other industrial sectors, especially mechanical engineering and vehicles. Kodama (1985, 1986) points out that the expression 'mechatronics' was first coined in Japan in 1975 and that even before that in 1971 an explicit policy designed to induce 'fusion' was initiated with the 'Law on Temporary Measures for the Development of Specific Machinery and Electronics Industries' which spoke of 'consolidation of machinery and electronics into one', and 'systematization' of them.

The highly successful Japanese development of robotics, CNC machine tools and flexible manufacturing systems also owes a great deal to the group structure of Japanese industry. The collaboration of the leading Japanese vehicle firms with 'their own' robotics suppliers and similar collaboration with electronics firms in the same groups is one obvious instance.

'Fusion' innovation may be regarded as a special form of cross-sector diffusion of a new paradigm. Kodama shows that 'technology fusion' takes place in Japan as firms in several different industries increase their R & D expenditures in new product fields outside their own main existing output range. He was able to identify this as occurring increasingly since 1975 in the instrument, electronics, machinery and electrical machinery industries. The Japanese R & D data permit such analysis in terms of thirty-one different product fields, and his analysis of 'fusion' is typical of what could be expected in a country whose national innovation system is well adapted to the diffusion of a new paradigm across various industrial sectors.

In the long run perhaps even more significant is the Japanese infrastructural policy with respect to telecommunications. Both before and since its privatization the telephone utility (NTT) has pursued its programme of an 'Integrated Network System' (INS). This is envisaged as ultimately providing a connecting web for information services to private and industrial users throughout the country. It will 'put a digital broadbased infrastructure in place in anticipation of its uses, while simultaneously developing those uses through model programmes and pilot projects' (Borros et al., quoted in Arnold and Guy, 1986, p. 97).

This appears to be a much bolder strategy than that of most other OECD countries, which is largely based on responding to current new business opportunities and is therefore more conservative in the scale and scope of new infrastructural telecommunications investment. The INS concept 'represents a discontinuous shift in the character of telecommunications networks' since it will enable broad-band-width services using video signals or other forms of very rapid data transmission to use the same network as telephone services. It will ultimately permit a much broader range of new information service provision, linking computer and telecommunication networks as a digital technology. The Japanese strategy therefore tackles the key strategic problems of diffusing information technology both to the service and manufacturing industries and to household consumers. This is very far from simply 'deregulating' and 'privatizing'. It amounts to establishing a new 'regulation regime' as well as a new infrastructure. Clearly, infrastructural policies of this kind will have a considerable impact on the rate of diffusion of specific new services and products.

As Melody (1986) has forcefully pointed out, in all OECD countries during the 'era of "de-regulation"' more regulatory activity has been generated than ever existed in the so-called "regulation" era'. National and international policies will have an enormous influence on the provision of new services, on technical standards, on terminal and systems interconnection, in value-added network services (VANS), on the radio frequency allocation and on prices. Japanese policy has recognized the fundamental strategic importance of this regulation underpinning the whole change of techno-economic paradigm in the same way as an electric power distribution system of a highway network in previous periods. This idea also lies behind the strategy for information technology diffusion advocated by Mackintosh (1986) in his book *Sunrise Europe*.

Arnold and Guy (1986) point out that the Japanese INS strategy involves a huge investment and the development of a broad range of new equipment and software almost entirely by domestic suppliers. The programme was started in 1982 at the same time as the Fifth Generation Computer Programme, which has attracted so much attention and debate outside Japan. Both were indications that Japan is no longer just a follower country. In the case of the Fordist mass production paradigm, as Yamauchi (1983) insists, Japan was two decades behind but had the great advantage of following a production system already well-established in the US and elsewhere, and improving upon it. In the case of information and communication technology, Japan is increasingly blazing the trail. This was already evident in consumer electronics in the 1970s and is now increasingly apparent in capital goods, manufacturing systems, information systems and infrastructure.

The success of the Japanese national system of innovation in catching up and moving ahead of countries that had previously been leaders in information technology confronts these countries with a formidable challenge; this applies especially to the EEC. But catching up with Japan is certainly not an impossible task, provided European countries are prepared to make the same effort to learn from Japan as she made to learn from the rest of the world. Nor does this mean simply imitating Japan. Potentially, there are a variety of different social and institutional solutions to the problems raised by the information technology revolution and the diffusion of a wide range of new products and services. The Japanese solutions are certainly not perfect. In some respects Sweden has found equally good or better solutions.

The Swedish example is of special interest because this is a case of a small European country with fairly limited resources, but which is nevertheless among the leading countries in the production and diffusion of robotics and in the design and manufacture of telecommunication equipment and in computer applications generally. Sweden's successful diffusion of ICT has been achieved whilst maintaining excellent social services, a high degree of consultation with trade unions and safeguards for civil liberty. Swedish industry has made particular efforts to keep in touch with Japanese developments and in general to take the best from world technology. Sweden was also committed fairly early on to giving ICT a high priority and probably has the most advanced training and retraining system in Europe. This clearly demonstrates the feasibility of catching up with Japan and perhaps of doing better.

The key problem for the EEC appears to be the whole-hearted commitment to long-term strategic goals, and the development of an institutional framework that enables and encourages individuals, organizations and firms to take their own initiative towards the attainment of these goals. Whilst this certainly poses a great challenge for European institutional innovation, it is by no means so difficult as the problem confronting Third World countries in their efforts to catch up with the leading industrial countries. Here, too, probably the most critical problems relate to institutional changes which would facilitate worldwide diffusion both at the national and international levels.

68   *Chris Freeman*

REFERENCES

Arcangeli, F. (1985) Paradigm Lost. Paper presented to the Sixth Italian Conference on Regional Sciences, DAEST, Venice.

Arcangeli, F., David, P. and Dosi, G. (eds) (1988, forthcoming) *Report of the Venice Conference on Innovation Diffusion*, 3 vols, DAEST, Venice.

Arcangeli, F., Dosi, G. and Moggi, M. (1987) Patterns of diffusion of electronics technologies. Conference on Programmable Automation. GERTTD, Paris.

Arnold, E. and Guy, K. (1986) *Parallel Convergence*. Frances Pinter, London.

Arthur, W.B. (1985) Competing technologies and lock-in by historical events: the dynamics of allocation under increasing returns. IIASA Paper WP-83-90; revised as Center for Economic Policy Research Discussion Paper no. 43, Stanford, Cal.

Arthur, W.B. (1986) Industry location and the importance of history. Center for Economic Policy Research, Discussion Paper no. 84, Stanford, Cal.

Bass, F.M. (1969) A new product growth model for consumer durables. *Management Science*, 215–27.

Bradbury, F.R., McCarthy, M.C. and Suckling, C.W. (1972) Patterns of innovation, Part 1. In *Chemistry and Industry*, pp. 22–6.

Clark, J.A., Freeman, C. and Soete, L.L.G (1981) Long waves, inventions and innovations. *Futures*, 308–22.

David, P.A. (1986) Technology diffusion, public policy and industrial competitiveness in National Academy of Sciences. In *The Positive Sum Strategy: harnessing technology for economic growth*. Washington, DC.

Davies, S. (1979) *The Diffusion of Process Innovations*. Cambridge University Press, Cambridge.

Dodson, J.A. and Muller, E. (1978) Models for new product diffusion through advertising and word-of-mouth. *Management Science*, 1568–78.

Dosi, G. (1982) Technological paradigms and technological trajectories. *Research Policy*, 147–62.

Floyd, A. (1968) A methodology for trend forecasting in figures of merit. In J. Bright (ed.), *Technological Forecasting in Industry and Government*, pp. 95–109. Prentice-Hall, Englewood Cliffs, N.J.

Freeman, C. (1984) Prometheus unbound. *Futures*, 494–507.

Freeman, C. (1987) *Technology Policy and Economic Performance*. Frances Pinter, London.

Freeman, C., Clark, J. and Soete, L.L.G. (1982) *Unemployment and Technical Innovation: a study of long waves in economic development*. Frances Pinter, London.

Freeman, C. and Perez, C. (1986) The diffusion of technical innovations and changes of techno-economic paradigm. Paper presented to the DAEST Conference on Innovation Diffusion, Venice.

Freeman, C. and Soete, L.L.G. (eds) (1987) *Technical Change and Full Employment*. Basil Blackwell, Oxford.

Gold, B. (1981) Technological diffusion in industry: research needs and shortcomings. *Journal of Industrial Economics*, 247–69.

Griliches, Z. (1957) Hybrid corn: an exploration in the economics of technical change. *Econometrica*, 501–22.

Hollander, S.G. (1965) *The Sources of Increased Efficiency: a study of DuPont rayon plants*. MIT Press, Cambridge, Mass.

Horsky, D. and Simon, L.S. (1983) Advertising and the diffusion of new products. *Marketing Science*, 1–18.

Issidoridis, G. (1986) Optimal diffusion: a theoretical and empirical analysis of the diffusion of innovations. D.Phil thesis, University of Sussex.

Keirstead, B.S. (1948) *The Theory of Economic Change*. Macmillan, Toronto.

Kodama, F. (1985) Mechatronics technology as Japanese innovation: a study of technological fusion. Saitama University, Tokyo.

Kodama, F. (1986) Japanese innovation in mechatronics technology, *Science and Public Policy*, Vol. 13, No.1, pp. 44–51.

McArthur, R. (1987) Innovation diffusion and technical change: a case study. In K. Chapman and G. Humphrys (eds), *Technical Change and Industrial Policy*, pp. 26–50. Basil Blackwell, Oxford.

Mackintosh, I. (1986) Sunrise Europe: the dynamics of Information Technology. Blackwell, Oxford.

Mahajan, V. and Muller, E. (1982) Innovation behaviour and repeat purchase diffusion models. *Proceedings, American Marketing Educators' Conference*, pp. 456–60. AMA, Chicago.

Mahajan, V. and Peterson, R.A. (1979) Integrating firm and space in technological diffusion models. *Technological Forecasting and Social Change*, 127–46.

Mahajan, V. and Peterson, R.A. (1985) Models for innovation diffusion. Sage University, Discussion Paper no. 48, Beverly Hills, Cal.

Mansfield, E. (1961), Technical change in the rate of imitation. *Econometrica*, 741–66.

Mansfield, E. (1977) *The Production and Application of New Industrial Technology*. W.W. Norton, New York.

Melody, W.H. (1986) Telecommunication – policy directions for the technology and information services. *Oxford Surveys in Information Technology*, 77–106.

Metcalfe, J.S. (1970) The diffusion of innovations in the Lancashire textile industry. *Manchester School*, 145–62.

Metcalfe, J.S. (1981) Impulse and diffusion in the study of technical change. *Futures*, 347–59.

Metcalfe, J.S. (1987) The diffusion of innovations: an interpretive survey. Paper prepared for IFIAS Workshop on 'Technical Change and Economic Theory: The Global Process of Development', Maastricht.

NBER (1962) *The Rate and Direction of Inventive Activity: economic and social factors*. Princeton University Press, Princeton, N.J.

Nelson, R.R. and Winter, S.G. (1977) In search of a useful theory of innovation. *Research Policy*, 36–76.

Perez, C. (1983) Structural change and the assimilation of new technologies in the economic and social system. *Futures*, 357–75.

Perez, C. (1985) Microelectronics, long waves and world structural change. *World Development*, 441–63.

Ray, G.F. (1984) *The Diffusion of Mature Technologies*. Cambridge University Press, Cambridge.

Rogers, E.M. (1962) *Diffusion of Innovations*. Free Press, New York.

Rogers, E.M. (1986) Three decades of research on the diffusion of innovations: progress, problems, prospects. Paper presented to the DAEST Conference, Venice.

Rosenberg, N. (1975) *Perspectives on Technology*. Cambridge University Press, Cambridge.

Rosenberg, N. (1982) *Inside the Black Box*. Cambridge University Press, Cambridge.

Sahal, D. (1977) 'The multi-dimensional diffusion of technology'. *Technological Forecasting and Social Change*, 277–98.

Salter, W.E.G. (1966) *Productivity and Technical Change*. Cambridge University Press, Cambridge.

Schumpeter, J.A. (1939) *Business Cycles: a theoretical, historical and statistical analysis of the capitalist process*, 2 vols. McGraw-Hill, New York.

Sharif, M.N. and Kabir, C. (1976) A generalised model for forecasting technological substitution. *Technological Forecasting and Social Change*, 301–32.

Sharif, M.N. and Ramanathan, K. (1982) Polynomial innovation diffusion models. *Technological Forecasting and Social Change*, 63–87.

Stoneman, P. (1976) *Technological Diffusion and the Computer Revolution: the UK experience*. University of Cambridge, Department of Applied Economics, Monograph no. 25, Cambridge University Press, Cambridge.

Von Bertelanffy, L. (1957) Quantitative laws in metabolism and growth. *Quarterly Review of Biology*, 217–31.

Yamauchi, I. (1986) Long Range R & D, in C. Freeman, ed., *Design, innovation and long cycles in economic development*. Pinter, London, pp. 169–185

4

The Financing of Technical Innovation

Frits Prakke

By any serious definition innovation involves both technical novelty and utility. Every business decision on innovation must therefore rest on a new combination of technical feasibility and economic demand. But to realize this combination there must be a third input, namely some commitment of funds, hence financing in the broad sense, sometimes small and short-term, more typically quite substantial and involving a high level of uncertainty. The purpose of this chapter will be to analyse this allocation of funds to innovation from a broad economic perspective. It is interesting to note that financing has not received the attention of economists that it deserves as one of the three major inputs into the process of innovation. That minority of economists who have been interested in technical innovation seem to have concentrated their efforts disproportionately on the interaction between technical feasibility and economic demand as prime mover of the innovation process, neglecting the financial input. Analyses of risk capital have generally not gone beyond institutional comparisons between venture capital organizations in the US and other countries, particularly in Europe. Orthodox economic analysis has suffered on the one hand from concentrating on the allocation by large firms of funds to R & D, blessed with better statistical data but lacking in relevance to the broader activity of innovation. Similarly, the extensive literature on government spending on R & D suffers from an overemphasis of the importance of R & D for innovation as well as an overrating of the role of government.

Economic analysis has also been limited by the restrictions of a static equilibrium framework. It seems particularly inappropriate to limit an analysis of the optimal allocation of financial resources for innovation to welfare effects under static conditions, in particular the assumptions that the utility functions of consumers and the transformation functions of producers are well-defined functions of the commodities in the economic system. Therefore, pronouncements by economists on, for example, the optimal level of R & D expenditures, or the precise effects of technical change on employment, often lack relevance.

If we start from the more realistic and, certainly with respect to the study of technical innovation, more appropriate assumptions that transformation functions of producers are subject to change, that such technical change is not reversible but evolutionary, that product innovation leads to changes in consumer preferences, that the market is a mechanism for the discovery of new demands, products and methods of production, that such discoveries are made by competing entrepreneurs running risks due to incomplete knowledge and uncertainty, then a different welfare criterion is necessary. The market process should then be judged not just by the static process of allocation but, as Heertje (1987) stresses, by the dynamic allocation of productive resources, i.e. the efficiency of the market as a vehicle for the process of discovery (Kirzner, 1985). We must therefore look at the allocation of financial resources to the process of innovation from the point of view of its effects on dynamic X-inefficiency. Differently worded, we should look at existing mechanisms for the allocation of investment funds with the purpose of assessing their effects on reducing the rigidities in the supply of capital. This rigidity is, according to economists such as Freeman and Soete (1987), one of the major reasons for the inadequate rate of adoption by Western economies of new technology, particularly information technology, and therefore a major cause of present technology-related unemployment.

The question then becomes the evaluation of the quality, particularly in Europe, of existing mechanisms for the allocation of investment funds with respect to reducing dynamic X-inefficiency. There are a number of significant aspects to this question that we should list here, albeit without the guarantee of providing fully satisfactory answers within the limits of this contribution. They form, however, the question to which I believe our research should be directed if the present answers remain incomplete. First, we should know whether, given the parameters of present technological opportunities – quite likely to be different from those of fifty or even twenty years ago – the supply of finance for innovation on the capital market and within corporations is adequate to the demand for such capital. Simply stated: is the volume, structure and quality of the supply of venture capital in Europe a bottleneck in the process of innovation of firms dependent on such financing. And is the corporate strategy of large European corporations able to supply sufficient funding for its technically innovative business units. Are capital markets efficient with respect to the transfer of funds to economic sectors with a high potential for growth? The distinction between the capital allocation mechanisms in markets and in hierarchies implied in this question is an important one to which we will return. The next aspect is the dynamic efficiency of the allocation of capital to product versus process innovation. In the innovation literature of the past decades recurring themes are the inability of particular nations to capitalize on scientific know-how in the form of product innovation and to properly exploit product innovation due to inadequate manufacturing innovation. We should ask ourselves if the allocation of investment capital to product and/or process innovation might be behind these inadequacies. A further question to be asked is whether the efficiency of capital allocation mechanisms (hierarchies as well as markets) is sufficient in each of the different stages of the business cycle. Do they serve equally in times of 'sickness and health'? These questions are valid for the shorter business cycle as well as for the long wave, which has – at least hypothetically – interesting technology-related causes. Finally we should ask ourselves whether, given the inevitable inadequacies of markets, the government has a role, either as a supplier of capital to the process of technical innovation or in its function as regulator of markets, including capital markets.

1   THE DYNAMICS OF TECHNICAL CHANGE AND THE ENTREPRENEUR

For the sake of clarity we will start our discussion from the simple micro-economic case of a single product innovation, the combination of technical feasibility and a market opportunity for which an entrepreneur, acting under conditions of uncertainty,[1] decides to seek outside financing in the expectation of future profits. This is the case of the new-technology-based firm (NTBF) to which we can later add complications such as process innovation, diffusion and the possibility that the entrepreneur is not fully independent but manager of a business unit within an industrial hierarchy.

How important is this case of the individual entrepreneur creating new techno-economic combinations? It can be said that he played an eminent role in the early years of economic science in the theories of Marshall and the early writings of Schumpeter (1939). But the preoccupation of more modern economists with the rise of the large industrial corporation as dominant phenomenon on the supply side has until recently tended to neglect the entrepreneur in economic debate. Also, there are possibly good reasons for this neglect to be found in real-world technological developments. Since the 1920s industrial technology has been dominated increasingly by economies of scale, exemplified by 'Fordist' mass production in manufacturing and upscaling in process chemical industries and by Big Science developments such as large computers, aerospace and nuclear energy. Individual entrepreneurs were not in the vanguard of these developments. However, in the 1970s a fundamental change took place in the nature of the dominant technological opportunities. Increasingly

---

[1] Uncertainty must be distinguished from risk. While risk refers to a situation in which the probability of success of a number of alternatives is known, or can be reasonably well estimated, uncertainty faces the decision-maker when he neither knows the probability of success of his alternatives nor whether there might exist any number of other alternatives, which he has not even considered. Managerial decision-making in operational areas can generally be reduced to acting rationally and routinely upon risks calculable by experts. Relevant alternatives are known and information on probabilities of outcomes is obtainable at reasonable cost. In contrast, decision-making on innovation is generally done in the face of uncertainty (see Luce and Raiffa, 1957).

exciting new innovations were small-scale developments in the sense that large R & D organizations, large investments in manufacturing plants and costly distribution networks were often no longer a condition for many of the most exciting technical innovations. Examples are to be found in such fields as micro-processors, home-computers, software, biotechnology and new materials. Intel Corporation, founded in 1968, became within ten years one of America's major producers of micro-processors and other advanced computational devices. Nixdorf is a European example of a new-technology-based firm that in a few decades has grown to pre-eminence in the production of computers. More recently, biotechnology has been advanced by such independent start-ups as Cetus, Biogen and Genentech. At a more aggregated level we see that in computers between 1945 and 1969 innovative output in the UK was dominated by large firms. But during the period 1970–80 small firms accounted for 40 per cent of all important innovations (Rothwell and Zegveld, 1985). At the sectoral level there has been a strong relative performance by small firms as measured by employment growth, certainly a good indicator of innovation. In the US electronics industry in the 1970s a study of 325 members of the American Electronics Association (AEA, 1978) showed that new firms grew much faster than older firms. Firms less than five years old in 1976 increased employment at an average rate of 57.7 per cent versus only 0.5 per cent for firms more than twenty years old. Firms beween five and ten years old increased employment at the intermediate rate of 27.4 per cent.

The reason for opportunities for innovation by small and new firms is the particular dynamics of technical change. A study (Overmeer and Prakke, 1980) of new firms in the Netherlands looked at the technological dynamics behind the rapid growth in the number of software houses in the Netherlands in the 1970s. In 1969 a decoupling took place in the prices of hardware and software. Mainframe computer firms standardized their software programs, whereas the needs of the users became more specific, creating many opportunities for the growth of new software houses. Furthermore, mini-computer manufacturers concentrated on the production of hardware. Because of their lack of knowledge concerning the software requirements of the diversity of users, especially in the service sector, a new market for software houses arose. Finally, the development of the micro-computer, with its divergent applications, was responsible for the rise of system houses, producing combinations of hardware and software directed to applications in specific areas.

Such examples of particular dynamics of technical change offering opportunities to NTBFs can be found in a diverse group of economic subsectors. The composition of this group is subject to change due to new scientific discoveries, changing demand and processes of maturation. Economic research has traditionally been concerned with the question of whether new or small firms are more innovative than large firms. Posed in this general way, the answers tend to be inconclusive. For our purposes it is much more important to note that there are at all times, and in particular in this present decade, subsectors where new or small firms perform better from the point of view of dynamic efficiency. There is ample evidence for this proposition in the industrial history of the twentieth century. A good, albeit imperfect, indication of which (sub)sectors are presently in such a situation is given in table 4.1, which gives a portfolio breakdown of European venture capital firms representing approximately 75–80 per cent of the total market.

The NTBF typically comes to the forefront as an agent of change in particular sectors and in particular timeframes. Then the impact can be critical. It seems that at the present point in time, given the present configuration of technological opportunities, the NTBF has an important role to play. It is an important phenomenon in the analysis of the dynamics of the economic process. Its neglect in previous decades is largely due to the biases of the economic profession of that period.

How does technical change present itself at the micro-economic level of the firm? And how does this affect the management of the firm, in particular the need for external financing? A useful approach is the technology life cycle model as developed by Utterback and Abernathy (1978). It holds that over time most technologies go through three distinctive stages (figure 4.1) characterized by different rates of innovation or technical improvement.

The frequency of product innovation is high in the first, fluid phase and decreases steadily as the major design issues are settled

Table 4.1 Breakdown of aggregate portfolio of 244 European venture capital firms in 1985

Industry sectors	Percentage
Communications	5.9
Computer-related	10.6
Other electronics related	8.2
Biotechnology	2.6
Medical, health-related	4.1
Energy, natural resources	3.9
Agriculture	3.7
Chemical industries	3.9
Space and aviation	0.7
Industrial automation	1.9
Technology not indicated (e.g. industrial products, wholesale)	54.5
Total (3.2 billion ECU)	100.0

Source: EVCA, 1986

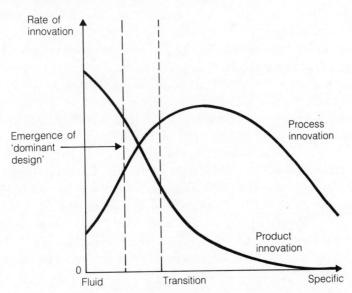

Figure 4.1 Frequency of product and process innovations in the stages of the life cycle of a technology.
Source: Utterback and Abernathy (1978)

in the second, transition phase, in which the dominant design emerges. In the third, specific phase the frequency of product innovations is low. The frequency of process innovations is low in the first phase, rises in the second phase due to an increase in the volume and standardization of production, and decreases again in the third phase, due to the gradual optimalization of the manufacturing process. As a technology matures the nature of uncertainty that the firm faces also changes, and with it the focus and strategy of its management.

Although, in its literal version, it is not equally applicable to every type of innovation, this model succeeds in combining economic, technological and management perspectives on the process of innovation. It models a dynamic which is also behind such corporate strategy concepts, widely used in industry, as portfolio management, which similarly classifies product–market combinations of firms according to the development phase of their technology. We return to portfolio management in section 4 below (p. 94). In each of these classification schemes (see also Hirsch's (1965) description of 'early', 'growth' and 'mature' phases), there is a useful characterization of the environment of the great majority of new-technology-based ventures, which face great commercial and technological uncertainty, compete on the basis of functional product performance, must maintain close links with scientific and engineering expertise, as well as to advanced users, and operate on a small scale at a low level of capital intensity. Nevertheless, its investment needs are difficult to fulfil, due to the high risk of failure and poor fit with the supply of capital, which is not accustomed and unwilling to finance intangible assets. Neither banks nor financial directors of large firms are generally capable of dealing with the types of uncertainty offered by investment decisions in this fluid phase of the cycle. While it is not impossible that NTBFs play a role in the transition and maturity phases of a technology life cycle it is in theory and in practice so exceptional that we choose not to discuss those cases at this point.

2   THE NEW-TECHNOLOGY-BASED FIRMS

An entrepreneur in the fluid or early phase of the technology life cycle seeking to obtain external financing on the capital market faces a number of obstacles. Having already cleared the considerable cultural and psychological barriers (Shapero, 1979) to taking the personal risk of starting up a new firm, a period of time must be bridged between the initial idea for a new techno-economic combination and the first sale to a customer. From that point it takes even more time until the break-even point is reached and until, at some further point in time, the new firm becomes established as a going concern with reasonably secure prospects. The duration of this venture development process depends on the nature of the technology and the market developments. It can easily be five years or even ten. For analytical purposes it is useful to distinguish the following stages: research and development, start-up, risky growth, regular growth and maturity.

Table 4.2 shows how in the different stages the typical activity of the firm and the type of likely sources of financing change. In stage 1, R & D, the firm has not yet been set up. Sympathetic incubator organizations such as universities may allow the entrepreneur to get a head-start by continuing employment and providing facilities at the beginning of this stage. Technical and commercial feasibility must be established. Specifications are to be drawn up. Market research is carried out to reduce commercial risk. Sufficient information must be gathered to produce a business plan on the base of which financing of the next stage can be secured. Even then, venture capital firms look seriously at only 10 per cent of the proposals submitted to them. In practice this stage may take up to a year and require an investment of up to ECU 300,000. The failure rate is very high, typically about 70 per cent. Financing comes from personal funds of the entrepreneur, such as savings or a mortgage on his home, or from family and close friends. Professional venture capital at this stage is rare, and must at least be quite specialist in the intended sector of industry. The reason is the very high technical and commercial uncertainty to be dealt with. The venture capitalist, if any, acts

Table 4.2 Stages in the development of a new-technology-based firm

Stage of development	Activity	Type of financing
1 R & D	Feasibility studies technical commercial;	Seed financing personal funds such as home mortgage family and friends
	technical development market research	new venture specialists (rarely)
(typical failure rate: 70%)		(typical investment: up to ECU 300,000)
2 Start-up	Further development; setting up production and sales; reaching break-even	Start-up finance venture capital
(typical failure rate: 30%)		(typical investment: up to ECU 1 million)
3 Risky growth	Further growth; developing a second generation of products	Fledgling finance (joint involvement of several venture capital organizations)
4 Regular growth	Achieving economies of scale in production and sales	Bridging finance (investment banks, venture capital, take-over by larger firms)
5 Maturity	Broadening technological base and management capabilities	Stock market or other exit route

almost like a partner and is likely to have considerable technical and entrepreneurial experience in the area of business. The local availability of such specialized venture capitalists has made areas such as Silicon Valley and Rte 128 around Boston into hotbeds of new ventures in microelectronics. Cultural variables are as important as technological and economic ones.

In stage 2, start-up, a firm is set up to carry out the business plan. A venture capitalist will usually become involved, providing management skills and area expertise as well as capital. His relationship with the technical entrepreneur can be characterized as quite delicate. He must judge technical, management and financial aspects in an environment that is characterized by a high rate of failure. Due to the high level of uncertainty personal trust is essential. This is reflected in the findings (OECD, 1985) that for 71 per cent of rejections of hi-tech venture capital applications the main reason was lack of confidence in the quality of management. The power of the venture capitalist over the entrepreneur is great and quite often resented. In this stage the cost of the innovation process starts to rise rapidly as the uncertainty starts to decrease, albeit at the cost of a high rate of failure (figure 4.2).

The typical failure rate of start-ups is a figure which necessarily rests more on expert impressions than on rigidly gathered economic statistics. It depends heavily on the definition of the population and on sample selection. However, it is generally taken to be about 30 per cent. Of every ten NTBFs, it is often said (Dizard, 1982; Gaultier, 1982), two prove highly successful, five become viable businesses of no particular note, and three end in liquidation. In a study of 200 American NTBFs spun-off from large NASA-related laboratoria, Roberts (1969) found that only 20 per cent failed in the first five years. Still it is probably a reflection on the extremely favourable market situation created by the procurement practices of NASA and the US Department of Defense at that time. In general, moderate success and failure must be regarded as inherent in the nature of NTBFs.

In stage 3, risky growth, the firm has a product on the market but still lacks a brand image, a sales network and in many cases a competitive manufacturing ability. In this stage such competitive features are developed, taking perhaps several years and a multiple

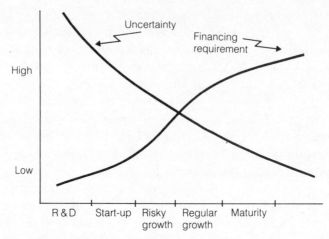

Figure 4.2 The development of the level of uncertainty and the financing requirement over the stages of development of the entrepreneurial firm.

of the previous financing requirements. The firm has established a successful product–market combination and hence represents a lower risk. But new venture capital is still needed. Insufficient internal funds are being generated and the assets are not sufficiently tangible to satisfy normal bank requirements. The major technical challenge is the development of a second generation of products. Very large amounts of funds are therefore needed. At this stage success can therefore easily lead to the failure of the firm. This period of cash flow shortage is therefore sometimes called 'Death Valley', typically occurring about four years after the start-up. To provide the increased amount of capital, joint involvement of several venture capitalists is necessary. Their role becomes more financial and less managerial.

In stage 4, regular growth, the firm puts further effort into developing a competitive production system and exploiting economies of scale. Technological exclusiveness needs to be protected by optimalization of product design through more formal R & D activities. In terms of the technology life cycle model of Utterback and Abernathy the firm is starting to behave according to the demands of phase 2, transition. Bridging or 'mezzanine' financing is sought, which may require a combination of venture capitalists and bankers. 'Mezzanine' financing (Baldwin, 1986) refers to those securities which are junior to debt but senior to equity in a company's capitalization. The availability of such financing is less dependent on the local and culturally determined availability of technology-wise venture capitalists and more on the general state of financial markets and cycles. The further development of the firm, which entails broadening of the technological base and developing the capability of replacing each generation of products with a new one, finally leads to stage 5, maturity, which opens the access to financing by means of public offerings of stocks. Even then, high-technology stock prices are characterized by an extremely high volatility, reflecting the underlying uncertainties of their profitability.

From the above description of the typical stages in the development of an NTBF a number of important conclusions can be drawn regarding the nature of venture capital. First, it should be recognized that from the point of view of dynamic efficiency the quality of this particular mechanism for the allocation of capital to technical change is based on a most sensitive relation between the entrepreneur and the venture capitalist. It is not fundamentally different from such relationships within industrial hierarchies where the innovative manager, sometimes referred to as the intrapreneur, is dependent on his relationship with an 'innovation champion' within the firm for obtaining the resources for creating technical change. But because the independent entrepreneur must go outside for his financing it is more evidently a market relationship. The allocative efficiency of this market must meet a number of conditions. There must be an ample supply of entrepreneurs as well as a sufficient number of potential venture capitalists. Furthermore, there must be sufficient, if not perfect, information at the disposal of the participants in this market. It is clear that such conditions are rarely met. In Europe particularly the scientific and engineering communities have been lacking in their ability to produce entrepreneurial individuals, probably due to academic culture and class attitudes. At present many European venture capital firms can be heard to say that there simply are not enough high-quality proposals for investment to meet their supply of capital. On the other hand, the supply of venture capital particularly in the early stages of the development of NTBFs is also lacking, certainly from the point of view of a particular entrepreneur looking for a financial partner with specialized technical and business expertise in his local community. The exchange of information between entrepreneurs and venture capitalists has been seriously hampered, particularly in Europe, by the traditional separation between the culture of the technologist and that of the banker.

On these points progress is at present being made in Europe, but it can safely be said that much still needs to be done. Many initiatives – such as the science parks that have sprung up near universities and the many new specialized venture capital firms – are now starting to make a contribution to this. Only when such initiatives begin to mature will the efficiency of these markets have improved. The sensitive relationship between technologist and banker, which is necessary to meet the information conditions of this market, can probably only be improved when a generation of successful entrepreneurial technologists leave their firms to join the category of financiers. They will then be in a position to aid aspiring technical entrepreneurs with capital and specialized management know-how.

Europe may take comfort from the fact that in the US also venture capital as an institution is a relatively new and surprisingly local phenomenon. It has taken quite some time to develop. The process of mutual learning and skill accumulation between technical entrepreneurs – initially university-based – and banks and other capital institutions started in the 1950s. The entrepreneurs only gradually went from a soft mode (technical consultancy and software) to a hard mode (selling equipment and standardized products to a general market) (Bullock, 1983). During this 'hardening' process the entrepreneurs had recourse to local sources of finance and established close relationships with them. At the same time local bank managers learned a great deal about technical entrepreneurs. Only in the 1960s did this culminate in the emergence of the professional venture capital industry, particularly in California and Massachusetts. In this latter state the venture capital network can be said to have played a major role in the intersectoral shifts of capital that transformed the economy from a stagnant one, based on such declining industries as textiles and shoes, to a flourishing one, based on semiconductors and medical technology. It is also interesting to note that metropolitan areas, such as Philadelphia and Chicago, similarly endowed with financial institutions and universities, did not spawn a venture capital industry.

With respect to the sensitive relationship between technologist and banker, Bullock (1983) states that due to the accumulation of knowledge during the past twenty years or so, many venture capitalists in the United States are now well able to assess the prospects of would-be entrepreneurs. Sophisticated numerical assessment techniques are rarely used. Venture capitalists claim that the key factors are a good understanding of the market and, most importantly, a correct assessment of the candidate entrepreneur. Market assessments are based largely on the new entrepreneur's business plan. The culture from which he or she comes, at least in the Silicon Valley and Rte 128 areas, is rich in accumulated experience available to assist in formulating such a plan. Whiston (1983) lists frequent mistakes made in the relation between technologist and banker.

1 In immature, rapidly developing areas of technology such as microelectronics, optical fibre technology, lasers, computer systems and biotechnology, assessment of proposals is very difficult for non-specialized bankers, as is judging the general growth potential of that area.
2 Considerable communication problems and misjudgements can occur on assessing the business/marketing aspect. Financiers will place over-reliance on accounting procedure and mentality. The candidate entrepreneur will overestimate the importance of the technical qualities of his new product to the detriment of market assessment. There is a mismatch of priorities due to the differences between the two cultures. Proverbial is the disagreement between the venture capitalist who wants to sell the products in order to create the necessary cash flow versus the technologist who wants first to complete technical development to perfection.

A final important lesson to be drawn from the description of the stages of development of an NTBF in table 4.2 is that the different types of financing represented in the third column are as links in a chain. The weakest link determines the performance of the whole. If the stock market does not easily accept new issues of stock, bridging or mezzanine finance becomes unattractive and will not be offered. Start-up financing is critically dependent on a good supply of would-be entrepreneurs with fully developed business plans. Only then can start-up financing evolve as a separate, specialized function. If start-up venture capitalists cannot after some limited period of time sell their interest to investment banks or similar institutions – including industrial conglomerates seeking to add to their portfolio of business units – then they will not have new funds to engage in their speciality, the financing of start-ups. In the next section we will therefore look at the institutional diversity of the venture capital market.

3   THE VENTURE CAPITAL MARKET

Venture capital can best be defined as capital committed, as shareholdings, for the formation and setting up of small firms specializing in new ideas or new technologies. Venture capitalism in this sense is not solely an injection of funds into a new firm; it is also an input of the skills needed to set the firm up, design its marketing strategy, organize and manage it (OECD, 1985, p. 13). Profit is sought not from dividends but from capital gains at the time of divestment. Venture capitalism defined more generally may be as old as capitalist production itself. Who first financed the trade with the Indies? Where did the funds to allow James Watt to develop the steam engine come from? But in its modern form as defined above it is generally traced back to the Rockefeller family, who started a special fund (Venrock) in the 1950s to finance the formation of new technology companies, or to American Research and Development (ARD), set up in 1946 at MIT by Georges Doriot to finance the commercialization of advanced technology developed at the major US universities. In the last two decades significant increases in volume have occurred. During most of the 1970s about $100 million to $200 million a year of new money came into the US venture capital community, but recently that figure has risen to between $2 billion and $4 billion a year (Perry, 1986). The size of the industry is relatively small in relation to overall investments. For the year 1981 Pratt (1982) estimated it at less than one-tenth of one per cent of pension fund assets.

In Europe similar growth is now taking place. The European Venture Capital Association (EVCA, 1986) estimates the total fund size per December 1985 at more than MECU 6590, and 38 per cent higher than the year before. As definitions differ and data gathering in this area is problematical at best, such figures should in any case only be seen as general indications of volume and trends.

The following categories of venture capital firms can usefully be distinguished (OECD, 1985, p. 16).

3.1 Individual Professional Venture Capitalists

This is the category most commonly mentioned and romanticized, but in terms of volume not the most important one. It consists of individuals, including former entrepreneurs, who have sufficient funds and skills to risk their personal fortune in this activity. This group is thought to have invested a total of $500 miliion in the US market up to 1981. The importance of non-professional providers of venture capital, such as family and friends, should, of course, not be underestimated.

3.2 High-Technology Investment Funds

These make up the largest category in the venture capital market. They are finance pools especially devised to operate in this market. Each is funded by a number of backers (typically with individual shares of $200–750,000 in a total of $6–7 million or more) and is managed by partners who receive a commission on profits. The backers are usually traditional finance institutions. Thirty per cent of the inflow comes from pension funds. A recent relaxation in pension regulations allows the large US pension funds to invest up to 5 per cent of assets in professionally managed venture capital partnerships and this is expected to increase their involvement in venture capital markets further. The partners, who control considerably larger amounts than the individual venture capitalists, are rare experts. They come from extremely varied backgrounds – management, engineering, law, journalism, etc. – with bankers, significantly, being very much under-represented.

The fact that the most prominent venture capitalists use funds from the traditional finance institutions reflects the chief feature of venture capitalism. It is more than the provision of high-risk capital in exchange for high potential returns; it is also the provision of special skills in identifying, evaluating and 'piloting' firms working with new technology. So venture capitalists seem to be far less financiers than suppliers of a highly skilled and specialized financial intermediation service. In mid-1983 there were apparently more than 400 high-technology investment pools in the US, about 200 of them being very active. Up to 1981 they are thought to have invested between $1.6 billion and $2.5 billion. In mid-1984, twenty to thirty of them were thought to have raised $100 million of equity capital per partnership.

A recent trend, resulting from their success, is for some of these high-technology funds in turn to become joint stock companies, with a market quotation. They can thus collect larger amounts of capital (between $15 and $100 million) and, by investing in more ventures, they can diversify and so reduce their risk. This procedure also reduces their chances of spectacular returns. It has been noted that funds with over 30 investment projects have an average rate of return very close to the average for all venture capital operations in the US. Leading companies are Merrill Lynch Venture Partners (set up in March 1983, collecting $830 million within a few months), Fidelity Technology Fund (capital: $700 million), Twentieth Century Ultra ($500 million), Alliance Technology Fund ($180 million) and Constellation Growth Trend ($165 million).

3.3 Small-Business Investment Corporations – SBICs

These are finance companies in the US that are regulated and licensed by the Federal Government. They can borrow up to three times their capital from government agencies, and their role is to support the creation and competitiveness of small business. Numbering between 350 and 400 throughout the US, they are thought to have invested $1–1.5 billion in ventures up to 1981.

However, most SBIC investment goes to small, family-owned service retailers, and only a very small percentage to high-technology companies. In Europe the many, mostly quite recently created regional development or otherwise government-sponsored participation companies might be called this continent's counter-part to the SBICs. Government sponsorship ranges from outright funding to favourable tax treatment of any losses.

3.4 Investment Banks

This refers to the venture capital activity of the traditional investment banks. Venture capitalism still represents a marginal proportion of the banks' total operations, and of the venture capital market itself. It is possible, however, that structural difficulties among their traditional clients, and the growing importance of small high-technology firms, will encourage the banks gradually to expand their stake in this area.

3.5 Venture Capital Divisions and Subsidiaries of Large Corporations

A number of industrial groups have set up such divisions or subsidiaries in the last few years, particularly well-known examples being General Electric, Xerox, 3M, Exxon, Olivetti (in the US) and Acme-Cleveland. They are generally designed to promote internal markets in capital, technology and skills, in order to ensure that their allocation of resources to high technology is more flexible, more easily reversed and more efficient. This in fact represents a partial substitution of hierarchical coordinating mechanisms by internal market mechanisms. However, these divisions and subsidiaries also invest in outside projects, provided they are relevant to the development and technological diversification of their group. Their decisions thus depend on a mixture of financial yardsticks – like the other types of venture capitalists – and strategic and technological criteria. They carry considerable weight in the venture capital market: they are thought to have invested over $1.5 billion up to 1981. The recent trend for several firms in a given sector to set up R & D partnerships may be considered to belong to this category

Frits Prakke

of venture capital investment. However, spectacular failures, such as Trilogy and Storage Teach Computers, have recently dampened earlier enthusiasm. Perry (1986) states that, in general, corporate venture funds have not been very successful.

An important feature of all these categories of venture capitalists is their geographical concentration. More than 50 per cent of all US venture capital organizations are located in either California, New York or Massachusetts.

Based on a survey per December 1985 (EVCA, 1986), table 4.3 gives an indication of the volume of funds per category of venture capital organization in Europe.

In the same survey a breakdown is made by stage of development of the NTBF. Of total venture capital in Europe 3.1 per cent is applied to seed financing, which reflects the fact that this is not an important area for officially listed venture capitalist organizations or professional individuals. Seed finance must generally come from personal funds, family and friends, not reached by such a survey. A further 22.4 per cent of the surveyed venture capital is applied to start-up financing, 50.9 per cent to expansion financing (our category of fledgling finance) and 17.6 per cent to buy-out financing.

A number of conclusions can be drawn from the above description of the state of venture capital markets in Europe and

Table 4.3 Volume of venture capital funds in Europe by type of source

Type of source	Percentage
Private individuals	7.9
Corporate investors	9.3
Government agencies	20.9
Banks	23.3
Pension funds	14.4
Insurance	14.1
Universities	0.4
Other	9.7
Total (4937 MECU)	100.0

Source: EVCA (1986) survey

the United States. First of all, an impressive growth in the supply of venture capital has taken place in the last decade, first in the US, then in Europe. In Europe the growth in 1985 was 38 per cent! This growth has no doubt improved the chances of the NTBF to obtain external financing. The quality of the market for the financing of innovation has improved on the supply side. Although venture capitalists, especially in Europe, complain about the lack of worthwhile new ventures, it also seems that a new generation of entrepreneurs is fast increasing the demand for this type of financing. However, such cultural developments may take more time. Having said this, it should be pointed out that the supply of venture capital is highly volatile. During the 1970s relatively small changes in US taxation of capital gains caused great swings in the supply of venture capital. New trends, such as management buy-outs, corporate raiding or national debt financing, could easily reduce the volume of investment funds available for technical entrepreneurs in Europe.

There has also been a marked improvement in the structure of the supply of venture capital in Europe. The categories of supply of venture capital form a chain from seed capital to placement of shares on the regular stock market. Any weak link diminishes the efficiency of the whole system. In many European countries it was until recently almost impossible for a young or otherwise not well established firm to be admitted to the stock market. It was therefore very difficult to find adequate external financing for firms in the critical stage of development prior to maturity. This has now changed dramatically with the establishment of 'junior' or 'parallel' stock markets in most European countries, where, after the example of the over-the-counter (OTC) market in the US, such firms have been getting admission and consequently an economically justified valuation of their worth. This allows earlier investors to realize their capital gains, freeing them to invest in a new generation of start-ups. At the same time it opens up new sources of capital for the needs of the firm that is developing from a stage of risky growth to maturity (see table 4.2). This certainly seems a structural improvement in the supply of venture capital in Europe. On the other hand, it appears that true start-up finance is still weak in Europe compared to the US, where this has become a more fully developed and professionalized institution. In a recent study the Dutch Scientific Council for Government Policy (WRR, 1987), the official national think-tank, has concluded that start-ups and small firms find it particularly difficult to finance demand for capital in the range between about ECU 20,000 and 100,000. Existing venture capital firms in Holland only play a role after this first risky stage has been survived. A number of very recent start-up funds of some banks and regional investment funds have plans to repair this link in the chain.

A European novelty in the structure of the supply of venture capital is the heavy involvement of government, 20.9 per cent in 1985. This state venture capitalism – the creation of venture capital companies with public funds – may be open to question. The ventures funded in this way do not enjoy the all-risk commitment of their backers who in any case are not usually businessmen. European governments, only recently kicking the habit of supporting weak sectors of industry for short-term political reasons, may not be able to keep such considerations from distorting the mechanisms for the allocation of capital to new ventures. In the US the Small Business Administration has tended to suffer from undue political influence. The many regional development funds in Europe in particular are in danger of political manipulation. This might also have perverse effects on the formation of firms not qualifying for public support (OECD, 1986). Might not bad venture capital drive out good venture capital? It should be remembered that in the US NTBFs flourish not because of government investment aids but because of government procurement. On the other hand, the local base of many regional development funds may be the critical ingredient for producing a typically European structural innovation in the supply of venture capital.

A third aspect of the efficiency of the venture capital market, after volume and structure, discussed above, is its institutional quality. The flow of funds, in volume and structure, can be quite volatile and quantity should not be confused with quality. It takes more time to develop the quality of the institutions, determined by the collective experience and attitudes of technologists and financiers in improving their sensitive relationship, often local or in a specialistic techno-economic field. This, of course, is hard to measure. But there are too many accounts of new initiatives in promoting NTBFs, spin-offs from laboratories, innovation financing, etc., taking place everywhere in Europe, not to believe that some considerable cultural change has started to take place. Through the internationalization of venture capital firms US experience is being rapidly diffused to Europe and Japan (OECD, 1986). This will undoubtedly speed up the learning process. Such change is not volatile but lasting.

4 FINANCING INNOVATION IN HIERARCHIES

In the analysis above we have focused primarily on product innovation in the fluid phase of the development of a technology in externally financed firms. This is an exciting and – we would argue – important focus for the study of dynamic efficiency of economic systems. But there is more. The Utterback and Abernathy model of the life cycle of a technology shows that a different but important type of technical change takes place in the transition and specific phases. Mature firms play an important role in this type of technical change. The recognition of diffusion and incremental improvement of technologies, typical of these phases, as very important forms of technical change from the economic point of view (see for example Freeman's chapter in this volume), point to the need for analysing their financing. It should also be recognized that some fluid-phase product innovation occurs in mature firms. It is therefore important to discuss the allocation of investment funds to innovation in corporate hierarchies.

The allocation of capital to technical innovation in large industrial corporations is achieved by means of corporate strategies. These are subject to change – some would say subject to fashion – reflecting, we would say, however indirectly, the changes in dominant technologies and markets. In the first half of this century a generally accepted strategy in industry was to strive for economies of scale and control over resources by means of vertical integration. This was Fordism. As, in recent decades, the general economic condition has shifted from favouring sellers to favouring buyers, there has been a strong trend toward looking at the parts of large corporations as separate profit centres, or business units, fending for themselves in the market place with specialized product–market combinations. The smaller scale of recent advances in technology, such as microelectronics and biotechnology has reinforced this trend. A dominant strategic concept in allocating capital to innovation in large industrial corporations has become the portfolio management matrix, or one of its many close relatives. This was first applied by the General Electric Corporation in the US in the late 1960s. This matrix can be seen as a rough translation of the technology life cycle, discussed earlier, to corporate strategy purposes. It categorizes the business units of a firm according to the phase of their technological base into 'wildcats' (fluid phase), 'stars' (transition phase) and 'cash cows' (specific or mature phase). This results in an interesting approach toward financing innovation in corporate hierarchies. The 'cash cows' need to produce the excess cash flow to allow the 'wildcats' a high rate of failure and to allow the 'stars' to finance the capital needs of rapid expansion. Central to the progress over time from 'wildcat' to 'cash cow' is the development of appropriable technical knowledge on which the exclusiveness of the product in the market place can be based.

   In practice not all large firms are able or willing to act in this way. But if they recognize the technological component of the portfolio management strategy, it can be said that this is an apparently efficient method for facilitating the financing of innovation in corporate hierarchies. In theory it is also an excellent mechanism for intersectoral shifts of capital from stagnant sectors to high-opportunity sectors, especially if the corporation is sectorally diversified. Decentralized management of business units allows for the necessary development of specialized management approaches to deal appropriately with the different levels of uncertainty inherent in different technological environments. With respect to product innovation in the fluid phase of a technology life cycle, there seems abundant evidence that large corporations have generally not been really efficient. They have fared better at the more systematic improvement of products and manufacturing processes in the transition and specific phases. Portfolio management has been an improvement over the previously dominant strategic concepts of maximum economies of scale and vertical integration. However, there are large differences between corporations. The sensitive relationship between technologist and banker, indicated above as critical to the dynamic efficiency of the venture capital market, has its counterpart within hierarchies. There one sees the struggle between technically oriented innovation champions and financial departments for funding of innovation projects of 'wildcat' and 'star' business units. The trend in recent years has been from financially oriented strategies aimed at conglomeration, as exemplified in the 1970s by Harold Geneen's ITT, to more technology oriented strategies aimed at developing a firm's core business. This seems to be a recognition of the fact that the effective management of this delicate relationship calls for specialization.

It seems clear that the problem of efficiently financing big-firm innovation in the transition and specific phase is still not negligible. This should be the speciality if not the *raison d'être* of large firms. But in the last decade a number of spectacular failures can be listed: the steel and automobile industry in the US and in the UK, the chemical industry in Italy before its present radical restructuring. The effect of Japanese competition on these firms seems to be a reasonable measure of their poor dynamic X-efficiency. From such evidence it could be argued that economic research has placed an inordinate amount of importance on the differences in innovative performance between small and large firms. In practice there have been much more important differences between large firms in different competitive and cultural environments. Even the largest industrial hierarchies have been dependent on such external factors.

The external capital allocation mechanism for industrial production is an important factor in international competition. In particular, countries differ in the extent to which industrial firms must obtain financing from long-term capital markets. Rybczynski (1974) found that for the period between 1960 and 1971 this was between 40 and 50 per cent for UK and US firms, between 25 and 40 per cent for continental European countries and below 20 per cent for Japan. When stock markets put a premium on short-term results firms dependent on this type of financing are forced to seek short-term objectives. Technical innovation in the transformation and specific phase, which often calls for large amounts of capital with long pay-back periods, suffers. A good example is the consumer electronics industry, in which US firms such as RCA refused to make the necessary investments in their core technology of component manufacturing. They chose to import components from Japan to gain short-term profits at the cost of long-term competitiveness. European firms, such as Philips and Siemens, under less pressure from the capital markets, seem to have held up much better. Firms in countries which provide ample long-term financing through such mechanisms as investment banking can then gain the advantage in global competition. In a situation of increasing international specialization based on production costs and quality, as experienced in the last decades, even small initial differences in the dynamic efficiency of capital allocation mechanisms between countries can result in vicious and virtuous circles of industrial decline and growth respectively. Stock markets tend to be shortsighted, valuing dividends above long-term increases in the ability to exploit technology for achieving exclusivity in the market place. For example, Japanese industrial expansion has been achieved in the security of an abundant supply of low-cost and loyal capital. It is generally agreed that the loyal and long-term involvement of West German investment banks was an important factor in that country's industrial success compared, for example, with Great Britain (Rothwell and Zegveld, 1985). The differences in economic performance between countries seem better explained by such institutional factors than by the traditional economic variables, such as cost of labour or firm size.

Apart from intersectoral and international differences in the quality of the process of financing innovation in hierarchies, there also is an indication of intertemporal differences, related to the phases of the business cycle or, more generally, the peculiarities of specific industrial developments. It is such contingencies that are the rocks on which the attempts of economic research to make general statements about the effect of size of firm on innovative performance seem destined to shipwreck. Under some circumstances the large firms are clearly superior in producing innovation. At other times they can fail miserably. In the decade of the 1980s a new threat has appeared to the innovative capability of industrial hierarchies. Under the pressure of corporate raiders firms are ever more forced to produce financial results that appeal to the stock market in the short term. This is a serious threat to the delicate relationship between the engineer and the financier, in this case the corporate director of finance, looking over his shoulder at possible corporate raiders.

5   CONCLUSION

There are two main types of mechanism for allocating risk capital to innovation: markets and hierarchies. Markets principally serve small-scale innovation in the early phases of the technology life cycle and hierarchies serve large-scale innovation in the latter phase. Due to technological and economic developments in recent decades small-scale high-technology entrepreneurship as exemplified by NTBFs has increasingly become an important vehicle for innovation. Apparently fairly efficient venture capital markets have been created to accommodate this development, first in the US, but more recently in Europe. Much technological change, in particular in the later phases of the life cycles of technologies, remains large scale and dependent on decision-making within the hierarchies of large industrial corporations. The recent development of technology strategies in exemplary large firms has created at least the potential of dealing efficiently with the financing needs of such systematic and incremental processes of innovation and diffusion. One might conclude that the periods of economic stagnation in the 1970s and 1980s have stimulated mechanisms for financing innovation which were absent or relatively underdeveloped during the previous period of high sustained growth. The direction of the developments is therefore positive at present, although many of the new structures are not yet fully established and vulnerable to even mild changes in the economic climate.

To a certain extent, the efficiencies of venture capital markets on the one hand and allocation mechanisms within hierarchies on the other compensate each other through the process of competition between small and large firms in the market place. But, on the whole, Europe must still be concerned about the quality of both. Some countries are clearly more competitive in producing NTBFs, others in supporting process innovation necessary for competing in the international markets of products, based on large-scale technologies.

The question should not be whether small firms are more or less innovative than large firms. The economic system and present technological opportunities demand that conditions in Europe should allow each to play its own particular role to the full and be competitive. Neither can be neglected. Further institutional development of venture capital organizations in Europe, including the creation of – often local and specialized – cultures in which the relationship and communication between technologists and financiers can improve, remains a long-term goal. The increase in volume in the supply of venture capital is not sufficient, mainly because it is subject to volatile developments in the financial sector. Allocation of funds to innovation in hierarchies is threatened by the globalization of the stock market and aggressive take-overs which serve no discernible purpose from the point of view of dynamic efficiency. This process, if left unchecked, could put pressure on large European corporations to forgo long-term investments in process innovation, in favour of short-term increases in payment of dividends.

Governments in Europe, acting on the basis of a traditional involvement in industrial development, have played an important role in providing venture capital to industry in the last decade at the depth of an economic crisis, acting as an investor of last resort. This has been stimulating to the general climate for industrial investment in new technology in Europe, but serious questions can be asked concerning the ability of governments to make effective investment decisions. If it is true that the low point of the economic crisis has now passed it may be time for governments to reassess their role and switch to instruments such as tax measures to increase the flow of discretionary funds to independent investors, rather than increase their own role of involvement in the allocation of venture capital. In the end, governments can probably be more effective in setting the conditions for markets, including the market for financing innovation, than in being a party in these markets.

REFERENCES

AEA (1978) Statement before the US Senate select committee on small business, 8 February.

Bullock, M. (1983) *Academic Enterprise, Industrial Innovation and the Development of High Technology Financing in the United States.* Brand Brothers, New York.

Baldwin, R.H.B. (1986) A view from Wall Street. In R. Landau and N. Rosenberg (eds), *The Positive Sum Game*, p. 467. National Academy Press, Washington DC.

Dizard, J. (1982) Do we have too many venture capitalists? *Fortune*, 4 October.

EVCA (1986) *Venture Capital in Europe 1986, EVCA Yearbook.* VUGA, The Hague.

Freeman, C. and Soete, L.L.G. (eds) (1987) *Technical Change and Full Employment.* Basil Blackwell, Oxford.

Gaultier, L. (1982) Evaluation et venture-capital. *Analyse Financière*, second quarter.

Heertje, A. (1987) Hoofdlijnen van een integraal technologiebeleid. *Economisch Statistische Berichten*, 1986, p. 675.

Hirsch, S. (1965) The United States electronics industry in international trade. *National Institute Economic Review*, vol. 34.

Kirzner, I.M. (1985) *Discovery and the Capitalist Process.* University of Chicago Press, Chicago.

Luce, R.D. and Raiffa, H. (1957) *Games and Decisions.* John Wiley, New York.

OECD (1986) *Venture Capital and Information Technology.* OECD, Paris.

Overmeer, W. and Prakke, F. (1980) Nieuwe innovatieve bedrijven in Nederland. Working Paper, Studiecentrum voor Technologie en Beleid TNO, Apeldoorn.

Perry, W.J. (1986) Cultivating technological innovation. In R. Landau and N. Rosenberg (eds), *The Positive Sum Game*, p. 467. National Academy Press, Washington DC.

Pratt, S.E. (1982) The United States venture capital investment market place. In *Financing More Innovation at Less Risk.* EEC, Luxembourg, SARL.

Roberts, E. (1969) Entrepreneurship and technology. In *Factors in the Transfer of Technology*, W.H. Gruber and D.G. Marquis (eds). MIT Press, Cambridge, Mass.

Rothwell, R. and Zegveld, W. (1985) *Reindustrialization and Technology*. Longman, Harlow.

Rybczynski, R.M. (1974) Business finance in the EEC, USA and Japan. *Three Banks Review*, 58–72.

Schumpeter, J.A. (1939) *Business Cycles*. McGraw-Hill, New York.

Shapero, A. (1979) The role of entrepreneurship in economic development at the less-than-national level. Working Paper Series, Ohio State University.

Utterback, J.M. and Abernathy, W.G. (1978) Patterns of industrial innovation. *Technology Review*, 41–7.

Whiston, T.G. (1983) Employment generation: financing problems of new, small and developing computer software (and related applications) companies, mimeo, SPRU, University of Sussex.

WRR (1987) *Investeringen en de financiële infrastructuur*. Staatsuitgeverij, The Hague.

5

The Process of Financial Innovation: Causes, Forms, and Consequences

Patrick Artus and Christian de Boissieu

Financial systems have experienced a dramatic change over the last twenty years. Even if the pace and the precise nature of the change have been different from one country to another, the dominant impression is that of a convergence among OECD countries. The purpose of this chapter is to study the process of financial innovation. After the presentation of the different aspects of this process (new financial instruments, markets, technologies; deregulations; globalization etc.), the analysis focuses on the causes and consequences of financial innovation.

1 THE PROCESS OF FINANCIAL INNOVATION

The economic analysis of financial innovation refers to the Schumpeterian distinction between process and product innovations. In some cases, the distinction between the two types is clear. For instance, electronic fund transfers obviously illustrate a process innovation, whilst money market mutual funds represent a new financial instrument. However, in most cases new processes and products are so deeply intertwined that they cannot be disentangled (e.g. cash management instruments permit a complete integration of current accounts, time deposits, mutual fund shares, etc., due to the wide computerization of the financial sector).

1.1   Leads and Lags

Electronic money and payment cards (credit and debit cards) are being developed at about the same pace in the OECD area. Leads and lags mainly concern the creation of new financial instruments and markets. From the time-schedule aspect, we may divide OECD countries into three categories:

1   the leading countries, where the pace of financial innovation dramatically accelerated in the period 1972–74 and thereafter: mainly the US, the UK and Canada;
2   countries where financial innovation was rapid at the end of the 1970s, as a result of a 'catching-up' effect. In this category, we find France, Italy, Japan, etc.;
3   countries such as the Federal Republic of Germany and Switzerland, which have tended to lag behind, even if more recently they have been keen to diversify the 'menu' of financial assets. One wonders whether, in the field of financial innovation, there is something of a paradox in the case of Germany. Compared to the industrial and technological advance of the country, the financial innovation process has been rather limited in the FRG. This may be explained by the combined effect of at least three elements: the complete deregulation of deposit and lending interest rates in 1967, which removed some incentives to innovate; the 'universal banking' system, which had the same effect; the 'moral suasion' exercised by the Bundesbank on financial institutions.

The domestic and international propagation of financial innovation is accelerated by the globalization of financial markets, the presence of foreign banks and their financial institutions and by the absence of legal protection for the new instruments. Some new payment technologies can be patented, but, to our knowledge, the only example of a patent for a new financial instrument concerned the cash-management account (CMA), introduced by Merrill Lynch in 1977, and this example is the exception which proves the rule: the other brokers offered, after a short lag, similar packages to their customers, under different labels. The lack of a legal protection for financial innovation means that the advantage of the leader is a short-term one, and may explain the short 'product cycle' of many financial instruments.

1.2 The Main Features of the Financial Innovation Process

Until the end of the 1960s, in a period of low inflation rates and market interest rates, savers (households, firms, etc.) had to make a trade-off between liquidity and profitability. Either they held liquid financial assets, bearing zero or negligible interest rates, or they invested in market instruments (bonds, shares, etc.) which were less liquid but gave a better return. With the rise in inflation and interest rates in the early 1970s, investors sought to reduce the opportunity cost of holding liquid instruments, and looked for new instruments possessing a high degree of liquidity and bearing market interest rates. In the US, money market mutual funds were developed by brokers and some other financial institutions after 1974, in order to increase their market share in the fund-raising activity. With the adoption of the Garn–St Germain Law (October 1982), banks and savings and loan associations were given the possibility of offering competing instruments (mainly money market deposit accounts (MMDA)). In Europe, the development of short-term mutual funds has been just as impressive (e.g. the success in France after September 1981 of short-term SICAV (Sociétés d'investissement à capital variable) and other mutual funds).

Due to the action of a 'ratchet effect' (which can be interpreted in terms of 'satisfaction level'), disinflation in the 1980s has not reversed this evolution. Notwithstanding the decrease in inflation and nominal interest rates, the success of financial instruments combining liquidity and market returns has not dwindled at all. It represents one of the structural elements of the financial mutation.

Financial innovation is closely related to other structural changes:

1 *financial deregulation*, which means, among several aspects:

the phasing-out of regulations on interest rates,

the removal of exchange controls (see, for instance, the programme of financial liberalization in Europe for 1992),

geographical and functional despecialization. In all OECD countries, the historical frontiers between investment and commercial banking, introduced after the shock of the great crisis, are vanishing. One important element of the present debate in the US concerns the adaptation of the Glass–Steagall Act of 1933 to the new environment where commercial banks extend their securities-dealing activity, and the legal removal of the geographical barriers to competition embodied in the McFadden Act of 1927 (these barriers have been, *de facto*, circumvented by the development of 'regional compacts' etc.),

the transition, in most OECD countries, from *direct* monetary control (e.g. credit ceilings) to *indirect* procedures based on interest rate movements.

Financial deregulation is a complex move, since it is accompanied by certain kinds of renewed regulation. Debt crisis and bank fragility have drawn the attention of monetary authorities to the *modus operandi* and reliability of deposit insurance schemes and to the various components of prudential control;

2 '*marketization*', namely the growing dependence of the activity and profitability of financial institutions on interest rate conditions. The development of asset and liability management is the logical response to the extension of various risks: interest rate risk, default risk and liquidity risk;

3 *disintermediation*. Financial innovation proceeds by way of an extension of 'direct finance' mechanisms, to use the terminology introduced by Gurley and Shaw (1960): i.e. through the various compartments of the market (commercial paper, the bond market, etc.), establishing direct relations between would-be borrowers and lenders. Due to disintermediation, the banking system is partially crowded-out of the financing sphere, but, with the rapid

extension of credit lines and similar operations, it finds other profitable intervention opportunities;

4 *securitization*, a process closely related to disintermediation. The concept refers to the development of marketable claims and liabilities, as opposed to non-negotiable credits and deposits. Securitization has many forms, and is illustrated by the success of NIF (note issuance facilities), RUF (revolving underwriting facilities), MOF (multiple option facilities), etc.;

5 *globalization*, which arises from the conjunction of monetary and financial integration and deregulation and is facilitated by new information technologies and the consequent decline in transaction costs.

1.2.1 A Description of Financial Innovations

It is not practical to seek to present an exhaustive list of all the new financial instruments which have appeared since the early 1970s (not to mention referring back to the appearance of the Euro-dollar market in 1957, etc.). In some cases financial innovation is merely fiscal innovation ('fiscal allowances' are used as incentives to facilitate the success of some bonds or shares, etc.). It is often a marginal change in some of the 'characteristics' (in the sense used by Lancaster) of a financial instrument: maturity, tax status, indexation system, etc. However, we may try, somewhat arbitrarily, to distinguish the following categories (leaving new payment technologies aside):

1 *cash-management procedures*, using computers and new information technologies to reduce the opportunity cost of holding non-interest-bearing cash balances;

2 new financial instruments, associated with the *financial intermediation process* ('indirect finance'). These can be disaggregated into subcategories according to the following criteria:

balance sheet headings. For example, Hadjimichalakis (1982) proposes a distinction between innovations used for liability management, those related to asset management and those which are intended to reduce the average and marginal operating costs of financial institutions,

market segment concerned by financial innovation. The division between retail and wholesale banking is made in most countries on the basis of the minimum denomination of financial instruments. For example, in the US, repurchase agreements (RP) with large denominations developed in the 1950s, but it is only since 1981 that smaller-denomination RPs, available to private clients, have been issued. The retail/wholesale criterion is sometimes taken into consideration in the definition of monetary aggregates (e.g. in the US set of monetary aggregates),

degree of marketability of financial innovation. In many cases, as Silber (1975) emphasizes, the success of a new financial instrument is conditioned by the development of a secondary market for it. The attraction exercised by CDs, not only in the US, but also in Japan, France, etc., confirms that negotiability is one characteristic that is highly appreciated by the operators. However, non-negotiable instruments, such as NOW accounts or money market deposit accounts in the US, and similar instruments elsewhere, represent a large market share, which may even grow, with increased uncertainty about interest rates;

3 new financial instruments or techniques, introduced into the *traditional segments of capital markets* (domestic or international) and integrated into direct finance procedures. Included in this large and heterogeneous category, we find:

variable interest rate instruments (shortening the maturity is a quasi-perfect substitute for variable rates; it may be interpreted as a special type of financial innovation),

swaps,

new instruments on the primary bond market: deep discount bonds (with zero-coupon bonds representing the limiting case), serial zero-coupon bonds, floating rate notes, etc.,

hybrid instruments, intermediate between equity and debt: equity note units, participating loans, participating securities, certificates of investment, etc. Due to financial innovation, the border between equity and debt, and that between shares and bonds, is diminishing somewhat;

4   instruments or techniques in *new areas of capital markets* (and also related to direct finance procedures):

commercial paper market (not introduced in France and Germany until 1985, despite its growth in the US since 1960),

financial futures (in Chicago after 1972–75, in New York, in London with LIFFE after 1982, in Canada, in Sydney and in Paris with the creation of the MATIF ('marché à terme d'instruments financiers') in February 1986, etc.),

options market,

unlisted securities market, intended to increase the equity basis of small and medium enterprises. Such a market has been installed in London in 1980, in Paris in 1983, etc.

These four categories of financial instruments help to open up capital markets, by creating a continuum of financial assets (according to maturity, risk, etc.) and a more complete integration of banking and market activities (e.g. the growth of off-balance-sheet operations). They help liquidity and risk management. In general, it can be a delicate process to try to separate those two considerations. A financial future contract in some cases is used as a risk management tool, in other cases as a liquidity management instrument, depending on the situation and individual expectations.

1.2.2   *The Distinction Between Private and Public Financial Innovation*

In Anglo-Saxon countries, product innovation comes mainly from non-governmental sectors (banks, firms, etc.). It arises spontaneously and in a decentralized way. *Private* financial innovation is predominant. The monetary authorities only intervene *ex-post*, possibly to monitor the phenomenon, to adapt the definition of monetary aggregates to the new 'menu' of financial instruments, etc.

In some other financial systems, financial innovation comes mainly from the public sector. Public financial innovation corresponds to a centralized process. It generally results from the initiative of the public decision-makers, who either introduce the new instrument themselves, or place restrictions on the comportment of other parties. For example, the concept of public innovation reflects the situation in France and in Germany quite well.

De Boissieu (1987) analyses more deeply the content and the implications of this distinction between private and public financial innovation.

2   THE INTERPRETATION OF THE FINANCIAL INNOVATION PROCESS

2.1   The Theory of Constraint

The most influential theory of financial innovation has been presented by Silber (1975, 1983), and may be called the theory of constraint. It considers product innovation as the response of an organization (bank, firm, etc.) to the constraints placed upon it. The main constraints which generate innovation are:

2.1.1   Regulation

Many financial instruments are introduced to circumvent regulations that bear a high cost of compliance. This cost is not exogenous. It is dependent on many variables, for instance on the rate of inflation: in the US, the cost of compliance with regulation Q (no return on demand deposits, and interest ceilings on time deposits) increased dramatically in the early 1970s, with the acceleration in the rate of inflation. Ben-Horim and Silber (1977) have interpreted major financial innovations introduced by large New York banks during the period 1952–72 as a reaction to regulation. Those innovations were introduced after a jump in the cost of compliance with the regulation, with a lag between the incentive to innovate and the actual innovations. Kane (1981, 1987) interprets the process of financial innovation in terms of a 'regulatory dialectic': innovations are a reaction to regulations and, in their turn, induce changes in the regulatory framework. This dialectic illustrates the evolution of many financial systems.

The relationship between regulation and innovation is not monotonic, but rather is represented by a bell-shaped curve (see de Boissieu, 1987): above a certain threshold of regulation, the strict control (or the 'moral suasion') exercised by public authorities causes a gap between the amount of innovation desired by non-governmental agents and the actual volume. Under these conditions financial innovations are *latent*.

2.1.2 Competition

Market constraints induce financial institutions and non-financial agents to introduce new financial instruments. For example, in the US most of the new instruments during the period 1972–83 were the result of tough competition between New York brokers and traditional financial institutions (commercial banks, savings and loan associations, etc.). As we have seen, financial innovation loosens market constraints only in the short-run, due to imitation and propagation effects.

2.1.3 Risk

The dramatic increase in exchange rate volatility (with the passage to floating exchange rates in 1973) and interest rate volatility (in the 1970s, due to the volatility of inflation rates and implementation of new procedures for monetary policy), was and is still the major constraint faced by economic decision-makers. It has induced recourse to numerous instruments (swaps, options, futures, etc.), which reduce the risk at the micro level, but transfer it, at the macro level, from high risk-averters to moderate risk-averters or to risk-lovers. The sophistication of risk-managing instruments seems quite without limit, and this may raise some difficulty for prudential control: with the complicated structure of risk redistribution, it is not always easy to identify the final bearer of the risk.

2.1.4 Other Constraints

In the Anglo-Saxon countries, where private financial innovation is dominant, regulation, competition and risk management are the main incentives to innovate. For countries where public financial innovation dominates, these constraints have also played an important role, but they were complemented by the interplay of other constraints:

> the external constraint. Many European countries have had to adopt a 'follow the leader' attitude: due to the severity of the external constraint, they have been obliged to follow the leading countries just to maintain the competitiveness of their banking system, the role of their main financial centre (e.g. Paris, Milan), etc. In the perspective of 1992, German monetary authorities are aware that the future of Frankfurt as a financial centre will be affected by the diversification of financial instruments offered on domestic markets;

> the government budgetary constraint. In countries such as France and Italy the Treasury department has been led to promote new instruments in order to finance, through non-monetary means, public sector deficits;

> financing constraints bearing on certain categories of firms, i.e. nationalized firms, small and medium enterprises. For example, in France (but some other continental countries had a similar experience), several financial instruments were created by the Delors Act of 1983, tailored to nationalized enterprises and SME because they serve to increase the equity basis of the firm without changing the structure of the property rights (they completely separate pecuniary from voting rights).

2.2   Other Analyses

2.2.1   The Lancasterian Perspective

The theory of the demand for characteristics explains a demand for new financial products in the light of changes in the environment, especially the increase and diversification of risk. This approach is complementary to, rather than a substitute for, the constraint theory. Desai and Low (1987), considering points in the characteristics space (elementary characteristics being, in their analysis, liquidity and return), study the 'distance' between different points and interpret financial innovation as a means of 'filling the gap', i.e. reducing the maximum distance between actual points in the characteristics space. Using British data, they give an empirical content to their analysis.

2.2.2 The Contestable Market Paradigm

Perfectly contestable markets satisfy two conditions (Baumol, 1982):

1 entrants have no handicap relative to the incumbent (no cost discrimination against entrants);
2 the cost of exit is zero.

The first condition is valid when considering the market for financial services. Entrants have quite an advantage over firstcomers, since they may reduce overheads and operating costs (non-financial firms, new banks, etc., have been able to minimize overheads and therefore to compete efficiently with traditional banks). The second condition is less fully satisfied. Will the non-financial firms that have entered the financial services market be able to reallocate their equipment in other sectors when the profitability of financial services is too low, or will they have to bear a huge amount of sunk costs? The reversibility of costs is here crucial. Empirical data are lacking, but we think that the exit cost is low in many cases, without being zero. It would be fruitful to deepen the analysis of financial innovation in terms of the contestable market paradigm.

2.3 Thresholds and Reversibility of the Phenomenon

According to Porter and Simpson (1980), there is no incentive to innovate unless the opportunity cost of holding traditional financial products or employing existing financial technology exceeds a certain threshold. These authors consider a threshold associated with a 'ratchet effect' (maximum interest rates for the preceding periods etc.) in money demand equations.

Financial innovation is irreversible only to a certain extent. New payment technologies will operate and will continue to be incorporated quite independently of short-term economic considerations. Financial instruments remain in the system, even if the causes of their creation vanish. For example, financial futures markets would not disappear should interest rate volatility significantly decrease. However, the attractiveness of these markets and the number of contracts would diminish in this case.

The structure of financing has a large cyclical component. The growth of capital markets and 'direct finance' procedures has been favoured by the interest rate configuration resulting from the disinflation process, namely the high level of real interest rates and the expected drop in nominal rates. The reverse phenomenon may occur if there is any significant change in the interest rate configuration. Starting in the summer and the autumn of 1987, we have seen some forms of 'reintermediation' and a marked slow-down in the securitization process. In this partial reversal, expected rises in nominal rates have played a major role.

3   THE EFFECTS OF FINANCIAL INNOVATION

3.1   *The Theoretical Advantages and the Macroeconomic Consequences*

The creation of new products, the possibilities of insurance against interest rate risk, the improvement of liquidity and the increase in the number of market participants on the financial markets have, in theory, a number of favourable effects. The fact that all economic agents can have access to a wide range of financial assets, the reduction in the number of missing markets, the better allocation of financial resources are, in principle, welfare-improving. The increase in competition between banks and the fact that they have lost a part of their monopoly power because of disintermediation should lead them to realize productivity gains and to reduce intermediation costs. Finally, the creation of financial futures markets (and of hedging instruments, e.g. swaps, caps, etc.) has several advantages that have been demonstrated by the theory that operators with great risk-aversion can be provided with an insurance against interest rate risk, and therefore (in the case of an enterprise), it is best to invest more and produce more. The fact that the prices of futures contracts are made public gives information to 'amateur' speculators about the interest rate expectations (as well as on the expectations of other connected variables) of the well-informed 'professional' speculators; this is advantageous since it allows more economic agents to take decisions armed with a rational foresight concerning future economic developments (see Brennan and Ulveling, 1984; Grossman, 1977), permits an acceleration of the convergence towards rational expectations (Bray, 1982; Stein, 1986) and a better market efficiency in the sense of Fama (1970), i.e. a rapid incorporation in the market price of all available relevant information. Moreover, price volatility should, in principle, be reduced. Futures speculation differs very much from speculation on the spot market since it does not require a large investment in cash; a given change in the current or expected interest rate will therefore induce a much larger response in the level of demand or supply because of the increased number of speculators, which has a stabilizing effect (Artus, 1987a; Campbell and Turnovsky, 1985; Kaway, 1983; Turnovsky, 1979). Pagano (1986) shows that a virtuous circle can appear: a reduction in volatility and hence in risk attracts new participants to the market, which in turn reduces further volatility.

It is interesting to summarize those various theoretical consequences of financial innovation using the usual IS–LM model. Hedging possibilities and the reduction of price volatility on the spot market increase firms' investment, hence the IS curve shifts to the right, illustrating a larger demand for goods being expressed for a given long-term interest rate. The substitutability between money and bonds is increased, a number of new products with various durations being available and all economic agents having access to the whole set of financial assets (equity, bonds, bills, deposits, etc.) directly or through mutual funds. This implies that a change in the rate of return on bonds leads to a larger response of money demand, the LM curve becoming therefore more horizontal. What are the consequences of these evolutions on economic policy and activity? Production must be stimulated by the increase in investment and by the reduction of crowding-out effects (a smaller change in interest rates is necessary to bring financial markets back to equilibrium since the elasticity of money demand to interest rates is increased). Fiscal policy becomes therefore more efficient, since less crowding-out occurs, while monetary policy becomes less efficient because of the larger interest rate elasticity of money demand.

However, Tobin (1983) and Baltensberger and Dermine (1986) have shown that the fact that investors have access to new interest-bearing financial assets implies, if no regulation on the interest rates on bank deposits exists, that those interest rates will vary more. If the return on money holdings begins to fluctuate greatly, one can observe, on the contrary, a decrease in the interest rate elasticity of money demand that would imply that monetary disturbances have larger real effects. The evolution of the slope of the LM curve depends therefore on the tightness of the regulation on deposit rates and on the choice of the monetary aggregate (whether a narrow or a broad definition of money) that is controlled by the authorities, as will be seen below.

The detailed representation of monetary and financial mechanisms must also be modified. During the 1970s, the theory of the 'overdraft economy' was developed, particularly in France. According to this theory, the key mechanism is the formation of interest rates on the bank credit market, the bond markets being little developed or fully controlled by the authorities. The central interest rate is therefore the bank credit rate, all variations in the liquidity of banks have thus an influence on the whole set of interest rates. The creation of new financial instruments directly issued by borrowers leads to disintermediation, and moves the heart of the system into the money market or the bond market, where the direct interaction of lenders and borrowers determines the level of interest rates, the situation of banks becoming a second-order factor. Many advantages of financial innovation can therefore be envisaged in theory. Moreover, difficulties and dangers can be identified in three different areas: the evolution of banks; monetary policy; the size and allocation of financial risk and the stability of financial markets.

3.2   The Situation of Banks

Disintermediation affects both the assets and liabilities of banks. Firms or the Treasury directly issue short-term (e.g. Treasury bills, commercial paper) or long-term (e.g. equity capital, bonds) assets, while investors substitute shares of mutual funds for bank deposits. However disintermediation is perhaps not so important a phenomenon as it might appear, since new assets are mostly held by mutual funds, which also collect an increased share of household savings, and those mutual funds are often subsidiaries of banks. There is, in this case, simply a transfer of assets from the balance sheet of a bank to that of a mutual fund.

If disintermediation actually occurs, banks can react in several ways: they can purchase bonds issued by firms instead of granting credit; they can themselves issue bonds to compensate for the decrease in traditional resources (e.g. deposits). This evolution makes the yields of the assets and liabilities of banks more sensitive to changes in interest rates, especially since the market value of assets fluctuates. However, this is mostly due to accounting methods, since capital gains or losses on bonds (which are marked-to-market) are registered in the balance sheets of banks while credit always appears at its face value, whatever the changes in interest rates. Banks' liabilities would, in any case, have a more fluctuating cost, which would make their profits less dependent on the level of interest rates since the average yield on their assets and the average cost of their resources would vary in a parallel way (which is already the case in the US, see Szymczak, 1987).

Disintermediation leads to 'marketization': the fact that bank loans, bonds and bills become closely substitutable leads to a reduction in the cost of credit for those companies who have access to other forms of financing. The effect on the profit margins of banks is ambiguous: if marketization does not lead to too sharp a decrease in interest rates on bank lending, banks lose the customers on whom they did not make much profit (large firms) and keep those for whom the spread between credit rates and market rates is the larger (e.g. small firms, individuals); however, if a large share of credits is distributed at rates close to the money market rate because of marketization, the profits of the banks can diminish. In all cases, even if the average profit margin increases, the amount of credit distributed by banks decreases because of disintermediation, and their total profits can be unfavourably affected. There exists a danger that, in order to offset the effects of disintermediation, banks will grant credit to new customers with a larger risk of failure or will increase the cost of credit to borrowers who do not have access to other sources of financing.

A great heterogeneity of borrowing conditions would therefore appear between those who can diversify their portfolio of financial liabilities and others.

Banks will also have an incentive to obtain larger productivity gains (moreover, dealing with new products is less costly than providing the usual bank services) and to increase the share of the fees charged on off-balance-sheet instruments (such as RUF, NIF, etc.) in total profits: the outstanding amount of off-balance-sheet commitments exceeds 200 billion dollars (BIS, 1986). The development of those instruments may introduce various new causes of instability (for example imprecise appreciation of the risk taken by banks; use of off-balance-sheet commitments in the periods when financial difficulties arise) which contribute to the deterioration of the situation of banks. Initially, banks could draw large profits from the new activities. The contestability of those markets mentioned above, and the development of competition imply that more and more new financial institutions will enter those markets, and that, in theory, profits will vanish. A considerable decrease in the profitability and solvency of banks is therefore possible. It is interesting to notice that the share of fees in total bank profits is larger in the countries where financial innovation is less developed (46 per cent in Switzerland and 27 per cent in Germany, compared with 24 per cent in the US and 20 per cent in France).

Some of the services provided by financial intermediaries (risk-pooling through the existence of mutual funds, distribution of consumer credit) will be proposed also by non-bank institutions (insurance companies, brokers, large department stores) because of the contestability of those markets. All this could lead to a steady decline in the profit margins of banks (because of increased competition, marketization, the variability of the cost of liabilities) and to a movement towards specialization in more traditional markets (management of wages systems, distribution of bank loans) where no competition from non-bank institutions is to be feared.

3.3   Financial Innovation and Monetary Policy

In all countries except Canada, monetary policy consists mainly of the determination of a target growth rate for money supply; the composition of the monetary aggregate under control varies from one country to another: in the US, after the period of 'new operating procedure', when the money base was controlled, a pragmatic targeting policy, referring also to the broad definition of money, has been implemented; the narrow definition is used in Germany. Financial innovation makes the difference between money and other financial assets less clear-cut; broad monetary aggregates (M3 or L) include risky assets (e.g. Treasury bills, CDS, commercial paper) which are substitutable for long-term assets (e.g. bonds); interest-bearing deposits (NOW, super NOW accounts, money market deposit accounts) are proposed in many countries. Money demand behaviour therefore becomes unstable, the previously estimated econometric equations exhibiting very large biases (see Judd and Scadding, 1982; Atkinson et al., 1984; Fröchen and Voisin, 1985) because of the increased possibilities of substitution between money (broadly defined) and bonds. This instability of money demand behaviour has several consequences for the conduct of monetary policy:

> the demand for narrow monetary aggregates shows a large elasticity with respect to interest rates, since the yield on the other forms of money varies with market interest rates. On the contrary, the effect of changes in interest rates on broad aggregates becomes small and uncertain because of the possibilities of substitution with bonds (as can be seen for M3 sterling in the UK and for M3 in France). It therefore becomes much easier to control M1 or M2, while target growth rates for M3 or L must take into account the possible shift in portfolio composition between money and bonds. This evolution has both a favourable and an unfavourable aspect. It becomes easier to control the evolution of M1 or M2 through interest rate management, but the monetary authorities must rely on the changes in the optimal structure of portfolios and not on the control of the total amount of financing or of activity which, in principle, they should aim at realizing. Moreover,

the fact that broad monetary aggregates cannot be kept on course (for instance if more than one money target is announced) leads to a decrease in the reputation of the authorities (as has been shown by Kreps and Wilson, 1982 and Backus and Driffill, 1984), which can be very harmful if one believes, like Barro and Gordon (1983a and b), that the main purpose of the definition of target growth rates for money supply is to influence the inflationary expectations of the private sector.

The increased possibilities of substitution between money market assets and long-term bonds imply that the term structure of interest rates (see Modigliani and Shiller, 1973) becomes more rigid (see, for instance, Shiller, 1979 and 1981b and, for France, Artus, 1987b). Any increase in short-term interest rates that is expected to be permanent is quickly and effectively transmitted to long-term interest rates: the authorities can therefore more easily exert an influence on the real economy, for instance through the channel of investment behaviour. On the other hand, it is no longer possible to use the differential between short-term and long-term rates as a policy instrument.

An important issue, therefore, is the possible reduction in the number of instruments of monetary policy implied by financial innovation, especially in countries such as France, where most of the capital controls have been removed simultaneously. We have seen above that the whole set of interest rates is in fact a single instrument. Moreover, the level of interest rates cannot be chosen freely by the authorities. Increased international capital mobility considerably limits the autonomy of monetary policies (even if the tests of the links between investment and national savings presented, for instance, by Feldstein (1983) tend to show that even for the US capital mobility is reduced; it is, however, possible that it is close to being perfect for purely financial capital and that it is limited for the claims on physical capital (Frankel, 1985). Moreover, the increased size of the bond market makes the authorities fear that overly large fluctuations in interest rates would produce capital losses, which could lead portfolio-holders to considerably modify their real decisions (e.g. consumption, investment) or to get rid of their fixed rate assets. If international capital mobility primarily affects the market for long-term bonds, there appears to be an international transmission of the changes in long-term rates which constrains the choice of short-term rate by the authorities. Because of the unavailability of the usual instruments of monetary policy, they will perhaps have to use other instruments, which should, in principle, be assigned to structural policies (such as the rate of required reserves or various prudential regulations) for stabilization purposes.

The supervision of risks by the monetary authorities has become increasingly necessary. The development of off-balance-sheet items (e.g. NIF, RUF, FRA, swaps) implies an increase in the risks taken by banks and is not so easily measured as are the more usual bank services. This has been perceived by the monetary authorities. At the beginning of 1987, the Federal Reserve and the Bank of England decided jointly to calculate common ratios, taking into account the risk attached to the various balance-sheet and off-balance-sheet items. Increased supervision of financial markets was also felt to be particularly necessary to avoid the use of insider information (in that spirit the Securities and Investment Board was created in London after the Big Bang). Coordination of the supervision of banks and of the prudential decisions of central banks will be useful in order to impede financial operations being transferred to countries where banking regulation is less strict. Moreover, the fact that non-bank institutions, which the monetary authorities have no power to control, play a central role in the markets will certainly be a major issue.

3.4   Risk and Interest Rate Volatility

In principle, new financial instruments allow market participants to hedge against interest rate risk. However, two difficulties arise:

> the hedging possibilities are more limited than is usually believed. In particular, it is not possible to be insured against an expected change in interest rates, since it has already been incorporated into the value of the futures contract; it is only possible to hedge against unexpected changes, which means

that actual capital losses may be only slightly reduced by the existence of futures markets;

risk does not disappear, but is merely transferred from agents with a high risk-aversion to agents with a low one. Unlike normal insurance contracts, there is no instantaneous interest rate risk-pooling on financial markets, but a compensation over time while interest rates increase, then decrease again. The uncertainty lies in whether the agents who provide an insurance against interest rate risk on these markets can all bear the losses entailed by an increase in interest rates and then wait until the opposite movement brings compensating capital gains.

Disintermediation also modifies the allocation of interest rate risk and of the risk of borrowers' insolvency amongst the market participants. Individual investors face the risk of insolvency of the borrowers when they directly purchase the bonds or equity issued by the borrowers themselves rather than benefiting from the risk-pooling service provided by banks. This scenario has both good and bad consequences. The market value of bonds is permanently known, and financial difficulties faced by the borrowers are instantly revealed, unlike in the case of bank credit. It is also well known that deposit insurance is an incentive for banks to take too much risk (Dothan and Williams, 1980). If the liabilities of banks consisted mostly of assets reflecting their actual value, they might well be more efficiently managed. However, the behaviour of atomistic bond- or equity-holders in case of capital losses (e.g. due to an increase in interest rates, or a fall in the corporate profits) is not well known. Would they sell more suddenly than institutional investors? Would there be more danger of a breakdown of the bond or stock market than of bank runs (Diamond and Dybvig, 1983; Bernanke, 1983) in the case of a financial crisis?

In fact, the question of the lender of last resort (LLR) again arises. If banks hold the whole stock of fixed rate assets, an increase in interest rates makes them suffer losses which they can cover by borrowing from the central bank. Making individual bond-holders solvent again is not so easy. Of course, the existence of an LLR is the source of a moral hazard effect that induces banks to take too much risk, but it also impedes financial panic and contagion effects (Saunders, 1987).

Finally, Van Wijnbergen (1983) poses the question of what amount of funds can be invested in risky assets or risky projects.

Financial innovation increases the yields on less-risk assets (e.g. money market mutual funds). It is therefore not clear that the public will express an increased demand for bonds or equity issued by the corporate sector. It is also not certain whether or not firms would substitute purely financial investment for investment in physical productive capital.

As has been seen above, the creation of new markets (e.g. futures, options) is theoretically stabilizing, at least after an initial learning period. However, empirical studies sometimes confirm this result (e.g. Artus and Voisin, 1987; Cox, 1986), but sometimes attribute destabilizing properties to the opening of those markets (e.g. Figlewski, 1981; Froewiss, 1979; Simpson and Ireland, 1985). Of course, we are not discussing very short-term (daily or hourly) stability, but the stabilizing or destabilizing effects of those markets within the macroeconomist's horizon (e.g. a month, a quarter). For technical reasons (e.g. simultaneity of the renewal of futures contracts, 'eleventh hour' problems with computers) instantaneous volatility may well increase.

The usual theoretical result stems from the fact that the responses of speculators to variations in price are amplified and that more information is made public. The ambiguous conclusions of empirical studies led to an attempt to construct theoretical models designed so as to exhibit destabilizing properties of futures markets. Such results were obtained in two cases. If hedgers select much riskier projects because of the existence of futures markets, this existence can destabilize the spot prices (Newbery, 1987). That would be the case for instance if firms undertook riskier industrial ventures, or if investors included assets with a larger interest rate risk in their portfolios.

The above scenario has probably occurred, mutual funds having adopted a kind of management aiming at obtaining much more capital gains in the short run than a regular yield in the long run. However, this new behaviour of mutual fund managers results more from the development of these funds and of the bond market, which is of course one kind of financial innovation, than from the creation of futures markets.

The second case has been discussed by Hart and Kreps (1986), who show that speculation is destabilizing when an event with a low probability of realization can create a large disequilibrium on the spot market. Let us assume that this event consists of an exogenous increase in demand which results in a surge in the spot price. If there is a signal that this event will occur during the next period, speculators will buy on the spot market today. If it doesn't actually happen and if the signal disappears, they will sell all the previously purchased quantities; this leads to a larger drop in prices than if no speculation had taken place. This situation is frequent on the foreign exchange market when a low probability is given to the possibility that a currency will be devalued, and a high probability to the stability of the exchange rate (it is the 'peso-problem' illustrated by Krasker, 1980). It seems less likely on domestic financial markets where changes in interest rates are more continuous.

More worrying perhaps is the possibility that speculative bubbles (defined by Blanchard and Watson, 1984) may appear. They consist of deviations of the market price from its 'fundamental value' (defined as the discounted sum of the future coupons or dividends) which are self-generating: the expectation of future capital gains leads to a current increase in the market value which validates past expectations of capital gains. The market value then diverges (perpetually and exponentially in expectations) from the fundamental value. Evidence of these bubbles has been found in many markets (on the stock market, for instance, by Shiller, 1981a) and, though they can also appear in markets where participants are not rational (Frankel and Froot, 1986), their presence is in theory linked to market efficiency and to the rationality of expectations. Financial innovation which acts in favour of one and not the other could hence be the cause of fully erratic movements in prices.

4   CONCLUSION

The recent drop in stock prices naturally poses the question of whether financial innovation will last and whether it is partly responsible for the crisis which has just been observed.

It seems that the causes of financial innovation still exist and are even strengthened by the recent fluctuations in the markets. It also appears that the financial crisis stems both from macroeconomic disequilibria and from the malfunctioning of traditional markets (speculative bubbles on the stock market). It is therefore reasonable to believe that new financial investments will continue to develop and to hope that they will permit, in a period when traditional assets (e.g. stocks, bonds) inspire much less confidence, the reduction of capital losses by those who are wise enough to diversify their portfolios and to maintain a steady financing of the economy.

REFERENCES

Artus, P. (1987a) Marché à terme, options et stabilité du marché au comptant de taux d'intérêt. *Finance*, forthcoming.

Artus, P. (1987b) Structure par terme des taux d'intérêt: théorie et estimation dans le cas français. *Cahiers Economiques et Monétaires*, 5–48.

Artus, P. (1987c) Fixation de l'objectif monétaire et réputation de la Banque Centrale. *Revue Economique*, 807–35.

Artus, P. and Voisin, P. (1987) Le MATIF est-il un marché efficace? *Banque*, 279–82.

Atkinson, P., Blundell-Wignal, A., Rondoni, M. and Ziegelschmidt, H. (1984) Efficacité des objectifs monétaires: stabilité de la demande de monnaie dans les grands pays de l'OCDE. *Revue Economique de l'OCDE*, 162–94.

Backus, D. and Driffill, J. (1984) Inflation and reputation. *American Economic Review*, 530–8.

Baltensberger, E. and Dermine, J. (1986) Banking deregulation and financial stability, a European regulatory perspective. *Economic Policy*.

BIS (1986) *Recent Innovations in International Banking*, Basle.

Barro, R. and Gordon, D. (1983a) A positive theory of monetary policy in a natural rate model. *Journal of Political Economy*, 589–610.

Barro, R. and Gordon, D. (1983b) Rules, discretion and regulation in a model of monetary policy. *Journal of Monetary Economics*, 101–21.

Baumol, W. (1982) Contestable markets: an uprising in the theory of industry structures. *American Economic Review*, 1–15.

Ben-Horim, M. and Silber, W. (1977) Financial innovation: a linear programming approach. *Journal of Banking and Finance*, 277–96.

Bernanke, B. (1983) Nonmonetary effects of the financial crisis in the propagation of the great depression. *American Economic Review*, 257–76.

Blanchard, O. and Watson, M. (1984) Bulles, anticipations rationnelles et marchés financiers. *Annales de l'INSEE*, 79–101.

Boissieu, C. de (1987) Lessons from the French experience as compared with some other OECD countries. In M. De Cecco (ed.), *Changing Money. Financial Innovation in Developed Countries*, pp. 212–28. Basil Blackwell, Oxford.

Bray, M. (1982) Learning estimation and the stability of rational expectations. *Journal of Economic Theory*, 318–40.

Brennan, P. and Ulveling, E. (1984) Considering an informational role for futures markets. *Review of Economic Studies*, 33–52.

Campbell, R. and Turnovsky, S. (1985) An analysis of the stabilizing and welfare effects of intervention on spot and future markets. *NBER Working Paper* no. 1699.

Cox, C. (1986) Futures trading and market information. *Journal of Political Economy*, 1215–37.

Desai, M. and Low, M. (1987) Measuring the opportunity for product innovation. In M. De Cecco (ed.), *Changing Money. Financial Innovation in Developed Countries*, pp. 112–40. Basil Blackwell, Oxford.

Diamond, D and Dybvig, P. (1983) Bank run, deposit insurance and liquidity. *Journal of Political Economy*, 401–19.

Dothan, U. and Williams, J. (1980) Banks, bankruptcy and regulation. *Journal of Banking and Finance*, 65–88.

Fama, E. (1970) Efficient capital markets: a review of theory and empirical work. *Journal of Finance*, 383–417.

Feldstein, M. (1983) Domestic saving and international capital movements in the long run and the short run. *European Economic Review*, 129–52.

Figlewski, S. (1981) Futures trading and volatility in the GNMA market. *Journal of Finance*, 445–56.

Frankel, J. (1985) Imperfect capital mobility and crowding out in the US economy; imperfect integration of financial markets or of the goods markets? *NBER Working Paper* no. 1773.

Frankel, J. and Froot, K. (1986) The dollar as a speculative bubble: a tale of fundamentalists and chartists. *NBER Working Paper* no. 1854.

Fröchen, P. and Voisin, P. (1985) La stabilité des équations de demande de monnaie: le cas de la France de 1970 à 1984. *Cahiers Economiques et Monétaires*, 5–48.

Froewiss, K. (1979) GNMA futures: stabilizing or destabilizing? *Federal Reserve Bank of San Francisco Economic Review*, 20–9.

Grossman, S. (1977) The existence of futures markets, noisy rational expectations and informational externalities. *Review of Economic Studies*, 431–50.

Gurley, J. and Shaw, E. (1960) *Money in a Theory of Finance*, Brookings Institution, Washington DC.

Hadjimichalakis, M. (1982) *Monetary Policy and Modern Money Markets*, D.C. Heath, Lexington.

Hart, O. and Kreps, D. (1986) Price destabilizing speculation. *Journal of Political Economy*, 927–52.

Judd, J. and Scadding, J. (1982) The search for a stable money demand function. *Journal of Economic Literature*, 993–1023.

Kane, E. (1981) Accelerating inflation, technological innovation and the decreasing effectiveness of banking regulation. *Journal of Finance*, 355–67.

Kane, E. (1987) Competitive financial reregulation: an international perspective. In R. Portes and A. Swoboda (eds), *Threats to International Financial Stability*, pp. 111–45. Cambridge University Press, Cambridge.

Kaway, M. (1983) Price volatility of storable commodities, rational expectations in spot and future markets. *International Economic Review*, 43–54.

Krasker, W. (1980) The peso problem in testing the efficiency of forward exchange markets. *Journal of Monetary Economics*, 269–76.

Kreps, D. and Wilson, R. (1982) Reputation and imperfect information. *Journal of Economic Theory*, 253–79.

Modigliani, F. and Shiller, R. (1973) Inflation, rational expectations and the term structure of interest rates. *Economica*, 12–43.

Newbery, D. (1987) When do futures destabilize spot prices? *International Economic Review*, 291–9.

Pagano, M. (1986) Market size, the informational content of stock prices and risk: a multiasset model and some evidence. *CEPR Discussion Paper* no. 144.

Porter, R. and Simpson, T. (1980) Some issues involving the definition and interpretation of the monetary aggregates. In *Controlling Monetary Aggregates* vol. III, pp. 161–234. Federal Reserve Bank of Boston Conference Series.

Saunders, A. (1987) The interbank market, contagion effects and international financial crises. In R. Portes and A. Swoboda (eds), *Threats to International Financial Stability*, pp. 196–232. Cambridge University Press, Cambridge.

Shiller, R. (1979) The volatility of long term interest rates and expectations models of the term structure. *Journal of Political Economy*, 1190–218.

Shiller, R. (1981a) Do stock prices move too much to be justified by subsequent changes in dividends? *American Economic Review*, 421–36.

Shiller, R. (1981b) Alternative tests of rational expectations models: the case of the term structure. *Journal of Econometrics*, 71–87.

Silber, W. (1975) Towards a theory of financial innovation. In W. Silber (ed.), *Financial Innovation*, pp. 53–85. D.C. Heath, Lexington.

Silber, W. (1983) The process of financial innovation. *American Economic Review*, 89–95.

Simpson, W. and Ireland, T. (1985) The impact of financial futures on the cash market for Treasury bills. *Journal of Financial and Quantitative Analysis*, 371–9.

Stein, J. (1986) Real effects of futures speculation: asymptotically rational expectations. *Economica*, 159–80.

Szymczak, Ph. (1987) Taux d'intérêt et système bancaire. *Economie et Prévision*, 3–39.

Tobin, J. (1983) Financial structure and monetary rules. *Kredit und Kapital*, 101–28.

Turnovsky, S. (1979) Futures markets, private storage and price stabilization. *Journal of Public Economics*, 301–27.

Van Wijnbergen, S. (1983) Interest rate management in LDC's. *Journal of Monetary Economics*, 433–52.

6

Financial Market Structure and Regulatory Change

Helmut Mayer and John Kneeshaw

In recent years innovation and structural change have transformed the international financial markets.[1] Changes radiating from the main centres and deregulation have, in varying degrees, also affected the domestic financial systems in all EEC countries. Securities market transactions have increased at the expense of traditional deposit and lending operations by commercial banks. The use of new instruments, many involving off-balance-sheet commitments, has spread rapidly. Financial institutions have undertaken new operations outside their traditional field of specialization. Competition between institutions has increased and the volume of market transactions has multiplied. With barriers to cross-border transactions and the entry of foreign institutions decreasing, financial markets in individual countries are becoming more integrated.

Innovation has offered borrowers, investors and financial intermediaries new and more flexible opportunities for obtaining credit, for increasing their liquidity and for hedging interest and exchange-rate exposures. The cost of credit to some types of final borrower has come down and in many cases better returns have become available to savers. Innovation has been facilitated by the development of new technology and financial skills and has

[1] Innovations in the international financial markets and their policy implications are examined in more detail in 'Recent Innovations in International Banking', a report prepared by a Study Group established by the Central Banks of the Group of Ten Countries, published by the Bank for International Settlements, Basle, 1986. The present survey builds on that report, but the authors bear sole responsibility for the views expressed.

helped to accommodate large fluctuations in the flow of savings and borrowing domestically and internationally, thereby contributing to more efficient allocation of scarce capital worldwide. It has provided market participants with ways of coping with volatility in the economic and financial environment. Stimulus has also come from regulations and changes in them, and to this extent the advantages and disadvantages of innovation are less easy to evaluate. In some cases competition has led to a proliferation of new instruments and a loss of transparency or to a concentration of market power. Moreover, rapid financial change can strain the capacity of institutions to adapt and of management to retain control. For the supervisory and monetary authorities it raises questions about whether the stability of the payments and financial system might be placed at risk in the longer run and how the efficiency of macro-economic policy instruments might be affected.

In short, financial change has posed a number of challenges for the authorities. Competition has created pressures for deregulation and for the acceptance of new instruments, practices and market structures. The general tendency has been to liberalize or to abolish interest rate controls, credit ceilings, limits on the sphere of business, bans on the use of particular instruments and controls on cross-border capital movements, but also to strengthen supervision of the financial institutions and markets for prudential purposes. In many countries the authorities have actively encouraged innovation in the money markets and the modernization of capital market procedures. In the European Economic Community the commitment to further liberalization of cross-border capital movements with a view to establishing ultimately a unified financial market seems to imply a need to prepare for further large changes in financial structures in the coming years.

Section 1 below outlines the main trends in financial market structures, which are identified as securitization, the development of off-balance-sheet operations, despecialization and globalization. Section 2 considers the forces behind private demand for financial innovation of the kinds which have been prevalent recently – in particular, the development of new instruments for transferring price or credit risk and for generating liquidity, credit and equity. Section 3 reviews influences on the supply of innovations –

technological change, deregulation, competition and the institutionalization of the process of innovation – and raises the question of the momentum of the innovation process. Forms of deregulation and official measures to encourage innovation in EEC countries are outlined in sections 4 and 5. Finally, section 6 discusses the resulting policy issues relating to the functioning of the financial system. These concern mainly questions of allocative efficiency, transparency, the management and supervision of banks, the stability of the financial system, and the effectiveness of monetary policy.

1 MAJOR TRENDS IN FINANCIAL MARKET STRUCTURES

While the variety of instruments and techniques which have been born of innovation in recent years is very wide, some major trends can be readily identified. They include, first, the increasing use of marketable instruments; second, the growing importance of off-balance-sheet operations, including contingent contracts, and third, growing competition as financial institutions undertake new activities and enter new markets at home and abroad. Finally, partly as a result of these developments, the markets are becoming increasingly integrated internationally.

The trend towards securitization can be viewed as a process, evident in most markets in recent years, in which an increased share of credit flows passes through the securities markets. This may lead to 'disintermediation', that is, a loss of market shares by banks. However, banks themselves acquire and issue securities and, particularly in the international markets, their role as investors and borrowers in the securities markets has increased dramatically in recent years. In fact, in another sense the term securitization refers to the greater marketability of bank assets resulting, for instance, from transferable syndicated loans, asset trading or loan swaps and the packaging of mortgages or other loans into securities. Special features of the securitization process have been the extensive use in the international markets of long-term debt instruments with floating interest rates and the development in many national markets of new short-term instruments, such as certificates of deposit and commercial paper.

The growing importance of off-balance-sheet operations reflects increased trading in the markets for various types of hedging instruments, such as options and futures, forward rate agreements, and interest rate and currency swaps. It also reflects the new development of options and futures markets in many countries and the provision by banks in the international markets of back-up facilities for the issue of short- and medium-term paper.

One manifestation of despecialization is the increased presence of banks in the securities business. In some countries where banks have long been engaged in new issue activity they have only recently been admitted to secondary market trading on the stock exchange via participations in member firms. In addition, however, banks have shown increased interest in providing other financial services, such as insurance, and in some cases they have extended their lending activities in fields such as home mortgages, consumer credit, leasing and factoring, which were previously dominated

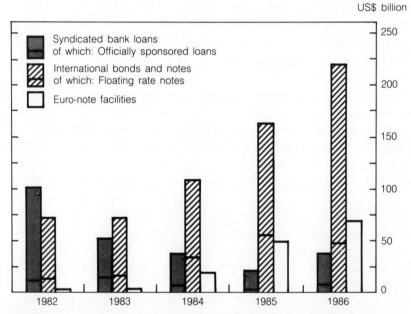

Figure 6.1 Trends in international financial markets, 1982–86. (Figures based on Bank of England data, recorded according to announcement date.)

by specialist institutions. In turn, traditional savings institutions have diversified into business lending. Along with the increased presence in many countries of foreign banks and securities companies, despecialization and the breakdown of traditional kinds of market segmentation have led to a sharp increase in competition in many fields.

Finally, the international integration (globalization) of the financial markets has owed much to the development of the international banking and securities markets. However, more recently it has received an additional powerful impetus from national deregulation and liberalization measures, as national financial markets were opened to foreign investors, borrowers and intermediaries. Changes such as the abolition of withholding taxes and exchange controls (see below) have increasingly blurred the borderlines between the national and international markets. In the field of NIFs and multi-component facilities, the grouping together under one hat of simultaneous borrowing options in the international markets and in various national markets has had essentially the same integrating effect. But even where regulatory and fiscal barriers or other types of structural rigidities persist, the use of the increasingly sophisticated swap technique has made it possible to exploit differences in relative borrowing costs, thereby drawing the national markets closer together. Finally, an important factor in internationalization has been the growing role of institutional investors, whose financial horizons, thanks to deregulation and securitization, have increasingly extended beyond national borders.

2 PRIVATE DEMAND FOR FINANCIAL INNOVATION

Although there is now a large body of literature dealing with financial innovation, there is still no generally accepted framework for analysing it. The changes involve both products and processes, but the distinction is not always easy to draw. Innovation in the narrower sense and quantum changes in the use of existing instruments or techniques may all be involved, and frequently it is a question only of the rediscovery of old products. Many innovations can be said to relate to the provision of insurance, arbitrage or options and permit the unbundling and repackaging of the risk characteristics of existing instruments (interest rate, maturity, currency, etc.). What is most evident is a pronounced increase in the number and diversity of new instruments. Views of innovation simply as a dialectic process that begins with a private response to inappropriate regulations, or as a process by which institutions give way to markets, are too narrow to describe the changes in financial structures that have been taking place in Europe. In practice, the only satisfactory alternative seems to be an eclectic analysis of the causes and effects of the changes.

The demand for new financial instruments can be thought of as deriving from an underlying demand for the characteristics of the innovations. Although it does not establish the kind of well-defined trade-off between prices and quantities for specific services that is customary in economic analysis, a classification of new instruments based on the type of intermediation function performed can be helpful in identifying the causes of financial change. Thus most recent innovations can be thought of as providing price- or credit-risk transferring, liquidity-enhancing and credit- or equity-generating services, although some new instruments, such as NIFs, perform more than one of these functions.

Price-risk transferring innovations permit the transfer between financial market participants of price risks inherent in financial positions. Options, futures, loan caps, swaps and forward rate agreements have all been prominent in the recent wave of innovations. Over a longer period there has been a shift to adjustable or floating rate loans and, albeit more rarely, price-indexed instruments have been developed. The principal influence here has been increased volatility of interest rates and exchange rates, both on a daily basis and in the medium term. Uncertainties resulting from inflation and large movements in real interest rates and exchange rates – due partly to excessive reliance on monetary policy to counter inflation – have been the main causes, along with significant changes in relative prices and other disturbances. But, in addition, monetary targeting and the floating exchange rate system and moves towards more flexibility in interest rate setting have also contributed to volatility in financial markets.

The demand for the credit-risk transferring facilities afforded by loan swaps, transferable loan contracts, credit guarantees of various kinds and securitization more generally was essentially an outcome of the international debt crisis in 1982 and the collapse of the energy boom. The resulting immobilization of substantial portions of banks' international assets, including a large amount of short-term claims, increased the need to improve the marketability and liquidity of the rest of their books, as well as the need for long-term funding. In addition, the deterioration in the quality of banks' assets reduced the perceived comparative advantage of banks in offering safety to investors and made it easier for prime non-bank borrowers to raise funds through securities issues instead of via the banks. Faced with this competition, and reluctant to expand their exposure to heavily indebted countries, the banks, in turn, responded by stepping up their role as guarantors of securities market instruments and by introducing new techniques for selling loans, either directly or after packaging them into securities.

Many credit-risk transferring instruments have also been liquidity enhancing, but, in addition, cash management programmes, money market mutual funds and new types of negotiable deposit accounts have been stimulated by the high opportunity cost of holding liquidity in traditional forms, especially under inflationary conditions. The potential loss of liquidity associated with increased use of capital market instruments has stimulated demand for increasing their negotiability.

Credit-generating innovations, such as liability-based interest rate swaps, 'junk' bonds and bonds with special currency, interest rate or conversion features, either tap new sources of finance or mobilize dormant assets to support new borrowings. In recent years one important source of innovation in the securities markets in many countries has been the large borrowing requirements of governments and the efforts of Treasuries to finance them by non-monetary means. Internationally, the shift of current-account imbalances away from countries which had turned mainly to the international banking sector to accommodate their external disequilibria towards countries which looked primarily to the securities markets has also created a demand for new credit instruments. On the borrowing side, the current-account deficits shifted from the developing countries, which had little access to the bond markets, to the US, which offered the favourite borrowing names in the international issues market. Similarly, on the investors' side the current-account surpluses shifted from the OPEC countries, which had deposited a very large part of their excess savings with international banks, to the industrial countries, notably Japan, whose preferred savings outlets were the long-term securities markets. In the domestic markets, too, an underlying factor has been the growing role of institutional investors placing savings flowing from pension plans and insurance. Another, transitory, influence was the constellation of expectations that emerged with the downward movement of long-term interest rates, which, on the one hand, encouraged lenders to attempt to lock in high yields with instruments such as zero-coupon bonds and, on the other, gave borrowers an incentive to refinance debts incurred under less favourable conditions. At the same time the recovery of the equity markets stimulated the use of bonds with conversion or option features.

Apart from the development of the technique of Euro-equity issues, equity-generating innovations have included new, typically non-voting, types of shares whose development has been fostered in many European countries during the past decade or so, mainly with a view to stimulating the supply of capital to small enterprises and new ventures, as well as instruments, such as perpetual floating rate notes, which were developed by banks in response to official pressures to improve their capital ratios.

A feature of many of the innovations worth stressing is the way they have permitted unbundling of financial risks. For instance, the negotiation of deposits or loans for future delivery could have provided protection against interest rate changes, but forward rate agreements perform this hedging function without necessarily involving a borrowing or lending operation. For a fee, options can place a limit on the interest or exchange rate risk of a possible transaction without imposing an obligation. Complicated series of swaps can, in effect, establish long-term forward markets in currencies. NIFs and RUFs provide back-up lines of credit for borrowers who raise funds through repeated issues of short-term paper with other intermediaries or in the market, and who need turn to the underwriting bank only if their notes cannot be placed or if increases in interest rates make their placement too expensive. Thus financing is separated from the provision of liquidity guarantees to borrowers and the protection of investors against interest rate risks.

3   REGULATION AND THE SUPPLY OF FINANCIAL INNOVATION

Although it is very difficult to determine when supply consider- ations are the binding constraint on financial innovation, forces that have increased the ability and willingness to supply new services in recent years can be identified. Apart from technological advances, these include deregulation, competition and the institu- tionalization of the innovation process.

Technological advances in telecommunications, data processing and display techniques have greatly reduced transaction costs and have increased market transparency. They have greatly contributed to breaking down the barriers between previously isolated markets and have considerably facilitated trading, adding breadth and depth to the markets. They have permitted market-makers to design and instantaneously price complex new instruments, to monitor positions continuously and to hedge exposures in new ways. International banks have increasingly been able to fit sophisticated and multi-dimensional operations into an overall exposure and earnings strategy. By sharpening competition and reducing the profitability of traditional lines of business, improved information has provided an incentive to the development of innovative custom-built products which promise, at least for a time, to give the innovator an advantage over competitors and to permit wider profit margins.

The provision of many new types of financial service has been facilitated by the general trend towards deregulation and liberalization in the industrial countries. The deregulatory momentum was in part due to the renaissance of free market philosophies and efforts to reverse the earlier tendency towards increased government control over economic developments. But another important influence was the desire to defend or increase the share of the domestic market-place in international finance.

As is discussed below, deregulation has encompassed a wide range of measures affecting domestic and international transactions and in many countries the authorities have played an active part in encouraging the emergence of new instruments, procedures and market structures. The trend has not been all one-way, however; in fact, deregulation itself has contributed to a need for improved prudential supervision of financial institutions, and in some respects this tightening seems to have inadvertently encouraged private innovation. In particular, though it was undoubtedly not the only influence, pressure from regulatory authorities, alarmed at the deterioration in the quality of banks' international portfolios, for improvements in gearing ratios seems to have encouraged the development of off-balance-sheet operations and an emphasis on expanding fee income from services, including securities operations.

The intensification of competition between financial intermediaries at the national and international level is partly a result of technological change and deregulation, which reduced the protection traditionally enjoyed in individual markets and areas of specialization. Technological advances created many opportunities not only for banks but also for large non-financial enterprises and institutional investors, permitting them to undertake new types of financial transaction and to monitor positions closely. One manifestation was the development of the 'in-house' bank. Moreover, in some countries non-financial enterprises, such as retailers, could seek to use their customer base to generate loan, deposit, credit card or insurance operations in competition with existing financial intermediaries. In many cases commercial banks, merchant banks, savings institutions and securities companies responded by attempting to broaden the range of their business so as to become 'financial supermarkets', though some sought to carve out market niches as 'boutiques'. In any event, pressures on the profitability of conventional activities were a powerful stimulus to innovation. With 'entrepreneurial' attitudes spreading in banking competition increasingly turned on the ability to create new instruments and operations, which, unlike technical innovations, could in general be quickly imitated by rivals. Particularly in the fiercely competitive environment of the international markets, being one step ahead of one's competitors in the development of new types of product has often been crucial in achieving good profit results.

This situation is reflected in the creation of 'new product groups' within the organizational structures of financial institutions. This might be said to constitute the institutionalization of the process of innovation in a way which tends to promote the innovatory impetus even if some of the exogenous stimuli should disappear. This new development might be regarded as establishing the financial equivalent of an industrial research laboratory.

Summing up, it can be said that the pace of financial innovation in recent years has owed much to temporary factors, such as the interest and exchange rate uncertainties associated with inflation and the subsequent deflationary process. Indeed, the pace of innovation seems to have slowed down somewhat since inflation has abated, though some earlier innovations, such as swaps, have continued to be used extensively. However, even if a degree of price stability is here to stay, it is likely, in view of the large fiscal and external current-account imbalances in the world economy, that considerable interest and exchange rate uncertainties will remain. Moreover, the momentum of the innovation process is partly due to irreversible factors, such as technological progress, intensified competitive pressures and institutionalization. The development of new computer hardware and software and the internationalization of the markets, reflected, for instance, in the growth of 'around-the-clock' trading, seem likely to continue, with international capital becoming increasingly mobile and asset diversification progressing. The spread of new instruments and techniques from the main centres to other countries, facilitated by deregulation, also is bound to go on.

4   DEREGULATION OF THE FINANCIAL MARKETS IN EEC COUNTRIES

The pressure of change in the financial markets, spreading from the main centres, has confronted the authorities in all countries with a need to re-examine the usefulness of traditional constraints on the activities of financial institutions and markets. Of course, the nature and scope of the established regulatory framework differed widely from country to country – some had long had fairly liberal regimes; in others official influence had traditionally relied less on detailed formal rules than on the sanctioning of private agreements and the delegation of authority to private bodies such as stock exchanges. Nor have changes uniformly been a response to private sector initiatives; in some countries the main stimulus has come from modifications to the rules and officially established procedures under which the financial markets function. In many cases the government or central bank has led the way in developing new instruments by changing the market operations used in government debt management or monetary policy. Fairly generally, too, there has been a tightening of the rules and controls in some respects, notably at the supervisory level, with a view to protecting investors and ensuring the stability of the payments and financial system.

The range of financial controls which have been removed or relaxed in individual EEC countries in recent years is broad; it includes credit ceilings, minimum bond investment requirements, controls on interest rates on the assets or liabilities of financial institutions, limitations on the scope of business, bans on the use of particular instruments, and exchange and other controls on cross-border capital movements. In addition, taxes that discouraged various types of financial market activity have been lowered or removed. At the same time, governments and central banks have actively fostered changes in the money and capital markets, encouraging the development of new instruments and markets and the modernization of procedures in existing primary and secondary markets.

Constraints on the asset portfolios of financial institutions, other than those of a prudential kind, have been removed in many countries which relied heavily on them in the past. Quantitative constraints on bank credit, for instance, were used in the early 1970s in virtually all EEC countries except Germany but are now used in only a few countries. Constraints on interest rates on bank deposits or loans are still in effect in some countries but have been substantially liberalized in France and made more flexible in Greece and Portugal. Compulsory investment requirements for banks have been considerably lowered in several countries, including Italy, and the scope of preferential credit-granting has been narrowed in some countries where it was formerly very wide. In most countries traditional mortgage lenders, savings institutions or the postal system have been permitted to undertake new types of lending and to use fund-raising instruments formerly available only to banks. At the same time competition has led banks to expand their mortgage lending, the UK being a notable case in point. Though equity participations are still restricted in some cases, banks in most EEC countries are now much freer to engage in securities operations than are banks in the US or Japan. In the UK, following the 'Big Bang', banks may operate on the stock exchange by acquiring member firms. Changes in the rules restricting stock exchange dealings to independent brokers are under way in France and are also under consideration in other countries.

Restrictions on the use of particular instruments, such as floating rate, zero-coupon, dual-currency, predictable maturity ('bullet') or very-short-term bonds and/or bonds with warrants, have recently been removed in some countries (including Germany and the Netherlands, where there were few direct restrictions on capital market operations). In many cases constraints on such operations as coupon-stripping, interest rate and currency swaps, 'drop-lock' issues or advance redemption of bonds have also been relaxed. Domestic currency markets for foreign bonds have been reopened in France and Italy, and in these two countries ECU issues have been encouraged by exchange control concessions. The incurring of ECU liabilities has recently been permitted in Germany. In recent years the issue of certificates of deposit has been authorized in Germany, France, Italy and the Netherlands. The issue of commercial paper has been permitted in France, the UK, the Netherlands and Spain. Tax obstacles to financial market activity have also increasingly come under review. For instance, withholding taxes on non-resident purchases of domestic bonds have been removed in Germany and France, and levies on new issues or on secondary market transactions in securities have been or are likely to be lowered in a number of countries. Others have taken steps to standardize the tax treatment of different kinds of placement or of placements at different kinds of institution.

Exchange controls were abolished in the UK in 1979 and have recently been substantially liberalized in France, Italy and Spain.

Controls imposed in the early 1970s to limit inflows of funds have generally been dismantled, and in Germany long-standing provisions designed to limit the holding of domestic currency claims by non-residents have also been abolished. In several countries greater scope has been given to foreign-owned banks and securities houses to participate as lead managers in domestic currency bond issues, to become members of the stock exchange or to operate in the domestic markets more generally.

5 ORGANIZATIONAL CHANGES IN THE FINANCIAL SYSTEM

The scope of the organizational changes in financial markets which the authorities in EEC countries have actively fostered is also extensive. It includes reform of the primary and secondary markets for securities, the development of new markets and institutions and efforts to foster structural changes in the financial system. Procedures in existing new issue markets for securities, including bond issue calendars and special arrangements for issues of notes or private placements, have been made more flexible. Over a longer period new types of government securities have been developed, many of which have subsequently served as a model for private sector issues. Examples seen in one or more countries, include zero-coupon, floating rate, price-indexed and partly paid bonds, new types of short- or medium-term securities and liquid savings bonds. In some cases Treasury bill markets, formerly restricted to banks, have been opened to non-banks, and auction procedures have supplemented traditional syndication or tender arrangements for the issue of bills or bonds. At the same time, the depth and breadth of traditional secondary markets have been increased by encouraging stock exchanges to accept new members with increased capitalization, to permit the merging of broking and dealing capacities, to adopt new technology, to coordinate their activities with other exchanges or off-exchange markets, to abolish or lower minimum dealing commissions and to extend trading hours. Over-the-counter and special markets with less strict admission and disclosure requirements or lower fees have been developed to facilitate equity issues by small companies and trading in these issues. In some cases secondary markets in government securities or mortgages have been reformed or new clearing arrangements for securities have been established. In a number of countries the establishment of new futures and options markets has been encouraged. Various constraints on the securities holdings of institutional investors have been eased.

In fact, far from impeding private initiatives, the regulatory authorities in many EEC countries have consistently sought to encourage and protect financial innovations in the domestic capital markets and have provided a strong impetus to change. In several cases a veritable transformation of the financial system has been achieved in this way or is in progress. In other EEC countries a liberal regulatory regime has left financial institutions free to develop new kinds of instrument freely in response to demand or to technological change.

6   POLICY ISSUES

Deregulation and financial innovation have raised a whole range of important policy issues. These can most conveniently be grouped under four headings: implications for the efficiency of the financial system, for transparency and for the supervision and control of individual financial institutions, for the stability of the financial system, and for the conduct and effectiveness of monetary policy.

6.1   *Effects on the Allocative Efficiency of the Financial System*

The innovation which has been taking place in financial markets should, in general, permit a more effective operation of market mechanisms. It has enabled market participants to choose from a wider range of financial products and to benefit from the reduced costs and enhanced protection they bring. In many cases, greater competition has reduced the cost of funds to borrowers and has raised returns to lenders as margins of intermediation have been squeezed – tendencies that should, in principle, lead to a more efficient allocation of available funds and to an increase in the amount of saving and investment. Liberalization has also tended to lower transaction costs for at least some non-financial market participants. It has given prime borrowers and, in some cases, small enterprises and even consumers, greater access to financing on attractive terms. Governments have found dependable sources of funds in the securities markets. To the extent that deeper markets with well-capitalized market-makers and homogeneous pricing have emerged, they can offer asset-holders greater liquidity. Liquidity and the variety of assets offered make it easier to tailor a portfolio of assets or liabilities to specific needs. New instruments permit the separation, hedging and spreading of different types of risk, which can, in principle, be transferred to those best able to bear them.

Advantages for individual buyers of financial services do not necessarily imply improvements in the overall efficiency of the intermediation process, however, given the inherent imperfections of the market and, in particular, the presence of regulation. The advantages of many types of regulation have, it is true, increasingly been questioned, but it is widely agreed that some rules are still needed, for monetary policy, for investor protection and to safeguard the soundness and stability of the financial system.

Innovation has not gone as far in some national markets as in others. In some countries regulations which fostered economic growth in earlier years by keeping the cost of credit to business artificially low remain in effect, but as the economy matures market criteria can become indispensable for allocating financial resources efficiently. Liberalization in domestic markets is often an inevitable concomitant of the freeing of international capital flows, and the latter offers the prospect of a better international allocation of capital and savings, particularly within a more integrated European financial market. In some countries the important question remains as to whether regulations or high costs limit the access of non-financial enterprises, including small firms in new industries, to the share and bond markets. In others, given that deregulation has brought an end to the setting of credit priorities, there is concern that, unaware of the risks, some borrowers who have been given greater access to credit, and in particular consumers, may be becoming over-indebted. Another area of concern is that short planning horizons in the financial markets, the institutionalization of capital markets and the tendency of enterprises to shift their borrowing from banks to the market may facilitate take-over activity and discourage productive investment. Financial reorganization of companies may increase the efficiency with which existing assets are employed, but the historical evidence suggests that this has by no means always been the case.

With respect to the newest types of instrument, a persistent source of concern is volatility in the markets. There can be little doubt that liberalized markets, in which participants benefit from new information technology, can be expected to respond rapidly to news. It is now accepted that under certain conditions this may increase the allocative efficiency of the financial markets, but there is less agreement as to whether behaviour in the financial markets merely reflects volatility in the environment or adds to it. Some ways in which the interaction of monetary policy and the markets may lead to increased volatility are discussed below. In addition, it has been suggested that programme trading and some of the new hedging techniques may tend to increase the volatility of the prices of the underlying instruments, though it is not clear whether they can influence price trends in the longer run. For instance, it can be demonstrated that some strategies such as delta hedging, widely used in conjunction with options, can in some circumstances accentuate exchange rate or interest rate instability. Although the empirical evidence is far from clear, it is conceivable that at times of turbulence delta hedging could become destabilizing.

6.2 Transparency and the Management and Supervision of Individual Banks

The bewildering array of new financial instruments, the increased use of off-balance-sheet instruments and the complexity of many of the new instruments give rise to problems of transparency. At the level of the individual financial institution, incorporating exposures resulting from the new instruments into overall risk and income strategies may overtax the ability of management. Some hedging techniques are mathematically complex. Some of the commitments entered into have no historical precedent and have not been tested in the courts. The extent to which banks may be called upon to honour commitments will depend in large measure on future macro-economic developments, in a way which cannot simply be projected from past experience. Despite the technological aids available, management has to rely increasingly on the quality and expertise of the staff. Securitization, which has dramatically increased the importance of the trading function within commercial banks, clearly demands talents and an outlook different from those of traditional customer-oriented banking and a greater emphasis on short-term risks and gains, which may also strain the ability of management to retain control. Increased riskiness of bank assets, on average, need not be a dangerous development if it is accompanied by higher earning margins, appropriate diversification policies and a stronger capital base, but there is a danger that, in a highly competitive environment, bank managements will not feel able, from the perspective of their own relatively short-term personal career horizons, to afford strict adherence to these principles.

Similarly, it becomes harder for supervisory authorities, who find it increasingly difficult to compete with banks for highly qualified staff, to evaluate the overall risk exposure of banks. The expanded role of banks in the securities markets is also a major challenge for bank supervision, which has traditionally focused largely on monitoring the quality of banks' credit portfolios in which, major accidents and sudden macro-economic upheavals aside, changes are generally gradual. In securities trading, heavy losses may be incurred in a matter of hours; no supervisory net is tight enough to monitor such developments in time. More than ever, the emphasis in supervision has to be on evaluating the quality of bank management and internal controls.

However, supervisors will also have to insist on full and appropriate accounting of off-balance-sheet exposures and will have to ensure that they are taken into account in calculating positions *vis-à-vis* individual customers and groups of customers. The ambiguities associated with many off-balance-sheet items make it difficult to attach a realistic weight to them for the purpose of computing capital requirements. A certain degree of arbitrariness will be inevitable, and supervisors will, if anything, have to err on the side of caution.

The Basle Supervisors' Committee, which was set up under the auspices of the BIS in early 1975, has been devoting considerable attention to the problem of banks' capital adequacy. A report by a subgroup of this Committee on the management of banks' off-balance-sheet exposures contains a technical glossary defining a wide range of such exposures. The aim of this glossary was not only to provide a common conceptual framework for discussion, but also to give some guidance with respect to the nature of the supervisory reporting systems about to be introduced in individual countries. Moreover, for the purpose of evaluating capital requirements, the report makes a distinction between categories of risk without, however, proposing specific weights:

'full risk', where the instrument is a direct credit substitute and the credit risk is equivalent to that of an on-balance-sheet exposure to the same counterpart;

'medium risk', where there is a significant credit risk but mitigating circumstances which suggest less than full risk;

'low risk', where there is a small credit risk which cannot, however, be ignored.

In early 1987 proposals for common minimum standards for the capital adequacy of banks in the US and the UK, including different weights for different risk categories of on- and off-balance-sheet assets, were published by the supervisory bodies in those countries. Specific weights for underwriting commitments in connection with NIFs have, moreover, been assigned or proposed in other countries, including France, Germany and the Netherlands.

The expansion of the role of the banks as borrowers and lenders in the securities market may imply that this market has substituted for the interbank market to some extent. This may be seen as a salutary development as long as it does not give rise to illusions regarding the capitalization of the banking sector. A large part of the paper issued by banks has been bought by other banks, but long-term subordinated debt will strengthen the capital base of the banking sector as a whole only to the extent that the debt instruments do not end up in bank portfolios. One supervisory authority has introduced rules to avoid the double-counting of bank capital. On a worldwide basis, however, such a policy may be difficult to implement.

Transparency is also, of course, of importance for other users of the published accounts of financial institutions, including shareholders, depositors and creditor banks. The limited informative value of published accounts was already a weak link in the working of the market mechanism before the recent spate of innovations. The growing importance of new instruments with complex and volatile risk characteristics makes a realistic credit assessment on the basis of published accounts even more difficult. This opens the way to various kinds of abuse and a misallocation of resources. It makes small investors all the more dependent on professional advice, which may not be disinterested, and may increase the preference of large investors for securities issued by non-banks. In any event, international accounting and auditing associations face a mammoth task of standardization and harmonization, which will be all the more difficult given the differences in national accounting principles and tax policies. The point is not whether particular exposures should be shown above or below the line, but that they should be reported as fully as possible and in a meaningful and consistent way.

In domestic securities markets traditional systems of investor protection which relied on collateral requirements for bond issues, strict eligibility criteria for stock exchange listing and the practice of large banks of marketing only high-quality issues (and of continuing to monitor the financial position of borrowers) have come under pressure as a result of competition or a desire to admit a wider range of borrowers to the market. There has thus been a general tendency to place a greater onus on the judgement of the investor, and in several countries new rating agencies have been set up, particularly in conjunction with the establishment of commercial paper markets.

The growth of the international securities markets gives rise to a number of statistical monitoring problems. Whereas information is available on bank intermediated credit flows, it is virtually impossible to trace the origin of funds supplied through the securities markets. Since, however, securitization reduces the relevance of banking statistics for monitoring international capital flows and indebtedness, efforts are at present being made by central banks within a BIS framework to complement the present international banking statistics with data on international credit flows through the securities markets.

6.3 *The Stability of the Financial System*

Deregulation and the development of the securities markets seem to have led to a weakening of the comparative advantage of the banking system, particularly as a channel of intermediation for high-grade borrowers. In turn, banks have moved more into off-balance-sheet operations. If these trends, which have been most evident in the highly competitive international markets, become more pervasive in domestic markets, there is a risk, first, that with high-quality borrowers increasingly turning to direct credit markets, banks will be left with the second-tier customers and that the average risk quality of bank assets may decline. Second, a decline in the banks' share in financial intermediation may also affect their capacity to play their traditional roles as shock absorbers and lenders of first resort in times of financial difficulties, and as transmission links for macro-prudential policies and official lender-of-last-resort operations. Third, this stabilizing role of the banks has been possible because they themselves had a vital interest in the health and survival of their customers, usually possessed an intimate knowledge of their customers' affairs and could exert a strong influence on their behaviour and policies. Fourth, agreement on common strategies is usually easier to reach when there are only a small number of creditors. In the capital markets, on the other hand, ownership of the debt instruments is typically widely dispersed, there are no long-lasting symbiotic relationships between creditors and debtors, and traditional lender-of-last-resort facilities do not exist. The absence of a close relationship between creditors and debtors may increase the danger of inappropriate use of the borrowed funds and the risk of accidents.

With respect to the implications of the recent wave of innovation for the stability of the financial system, several related points of concern are often mentioned. They include an over-leveraging of capital, the apparent underpricing of new instruments, the scope for an undue concentration of risks, and the possibility that the apparent liquidity of marketable instruments could prove illusory under adverse circumstances.

The increase in off-balance-sheet activities was in part a response to the tightening of officially imposed capital requirements, as these activities bring additional income without an expansion of bank balance sheets. Unless they are constrained by a supervisory effort, there is a danger that, in relation to the risks incurred, banks' own cushions of capital will become inadequate.

The trend towards over-leveraging may be reinforced by a systematic tendency to underprice the new instruments, with the result that retained earnings cannot provide sufficient protection against the additional risks incurred. There are a number of reasons why, in a highly competitive environment, the danger of systematic underpricing may be greater in new areas than in the case of existing instruments. To begin with, long-run profit maximization may give rise to efforts to secure market shares in the new instruments even if earning margins are thereby squeezed to an unreasonable extent. A lack of historical experience, and the fact that the probabilities are more difficult to assess than in the case of traditional credit instruments, may lead to an underestimation of the risks involved. Over-optimism in this respect may be encouraged by the link between the volume of business in the new areas and personal success and promotion. Finally, there may be a tendency to evaluate the risks against the background of the current macro-economic environment, without making sufficient allowance for the possibility of a fundamental adverse change in market conditions and in the associated risk covariances.

The banks' lending strategies with respect to developing countries in the five years before the outbreak of the international debt crisis provide a good illustration of a number of these points. Similarly, it is not clear to central banks whether, for example, the very low fees charged by the banks for underwriting commitments in connection with NIFs take into account the likelihood that, in the event of a sharp tightening of credit conditions, the banks would all be called upon to honour their commitments at the same time, and this at earning margins which might prove to be wholly inadequate in the circumstances then prevailing.

In addition to the dangers of over-leveraging and underpricing, there is the possibility of an undue concentration of risks. As mentioned before, a prominent feature of the new instruments has been that they permit an unbundling and transfer of market risks within the financial system. In particular, they may give rise to a transfer of market risks to the limited number of financial institutions which, in view of their expertise, feel qualified to manage them. As a result, the risks may be concentrated in a few hands. The writing of options is comparable to the writing of insurance for a fee; but there are two major ways in which option-writing differs from insurance and which make option-writing a much riskier business: the parameters, such as exchange rate volatility, are highly unstable, and the law of large numbers does not apply, as the covariance is of overwhelming importance. If, for example, the exchange rate moves in a certain way, all buyers of, say, a call option are bound to exercise it. With respect to some instruments such as swaps, another concern is that a multiple combination of risks in a chain of transactions can make it difficult to assess properly the riskiness of individual transactions.

The sharp increase in importace of securities in banks' own balance sheets may enhance liquidity in a favourable credit market climate. However, the increased liquidity may prove to be illusory in a context of rising interest rates or a major upheaval in the credit markets – and this at a time when the banks would doubtless be swamped with a wave of new credit demands from their major customers and would be called upon to honour commitments entered into at a time of slack credit demand. Moreover, in holding large portfolios of long-term securities banks join non-bank investors who, having no long-established business relationship with the debtors, may tend to be more easily alarmed and less willing to take long-term considerations into account. Furthermore, the markets for some new instruments may prove relatively narrow, perhaps because few have been issued, or because they are not close substitutes for more conventional instruments, or because the market is dependent on only a few sponsoring investment banks as market-makers. In these cases, too, the liquidity of an instrument may be only apparent – the failure of the market-maker or the desire of some asset-holders to divest may render the market inoperative.

Phenomena of this kind seem to have been factors in the failure of the market in perpetual floating rate notes in 1986. Experience has also shown that banks that rely heavily on liability management, while holding asset portfolios of less than prime quality, can be vulnerable to liquidity strains.

The replacement of loans by securities in bank portfolios has in some cases also had accounting implications, with very tangible economic consequences. Whereas the value of conventional loans does not have to be written down when interest rates rise, the situation may be different in the case of tradable assets with quoted prices. This could mean that a rise in interest rates might have to be quickly translated into reported losses even if the assets were not sold, with obvious consequences for the stability of the system as a whole and the authorities' monetary policy leeway.

At the national level the growth of financial conglomerates and the blurring of distinctions between banking and the securities markets may also raise questions about conflicts of interest in agency dealing and market-making, as well as problems with regard to the relationship between different supervisory areas. Diversification by banks into securities operations may reduce risks even if the securities industry is inherently more risky. In many countries banks have traditionally carried out extensive securities operations, using fee income to compensate for cyclical swings in the return on loan portfolios. Diversification may also be seen as a useful way of improving the liquidity of the securities markets, provided the regulatory net is extended to cover the full range of services. However, in some countries the existing supervisory framework in the securities markets tends to concentrate on investor protection, and there may be a need for a redefinition of supervisory responsibilities, perhaps on functional lines and with more explicit provision for coordination to reflect, in particular, the central bank's concern with systemic stability.

Affiliations between banks and non-financial enterprises may give rise to serious conflicts of interest. Some countries have not had to face issues of this kind, able to rely on broad legal definitions of what constitutes a bank, on requirements that banks be separately incorporated and on rules limiting concentrations of risk in lending. Even so, ownership of a bank by a non-financial enterprise may be seen as a potential source of risk to the bank – if only to the extent that any separation of functions fails to convince the markets. There is also a risk of the parent non-financial institution using the bank's deposit base to finance the parent group. The prospect of non-financial enterprises acquiring or operating banks or other financial enterprises has been regarded as a cause for concern in several countries.

It is widely acknowledged that the internationalization of the markets calls for international coordination of supervision to prevent the transfer of risks to centres with weaker prudential requirements. Internationalization of the financial markets is not an entirely new trend. The internationalization of banking and the related emergence of the Euro-markets were already important steps in this direction. These developments, of course, not only created new profit opportunities for the banks but entailed additional risks, tougher competition and new possibilities of losses. Moreover, by setting up affiliates in the international markets and booking domestic business through them, the banks were able to avoid many of the prudential restrictions to which they were subject at home, such as limits on risk concentration and capital gearing. This escape from controls, underpinned by the fierceness of competition for market shares, could ultimately have posed a serious threat to the stability of the international banking system. As already mentioned, central banks reacted as early as 1975 by setting up under BIS auspices an international Supervisors' Committee whose task it was to deal with the various problems raised by the internationalization of banking. One of the first aims of the Committee was to try to ensure that no banking establishment, wherever it might be located and registered, went unsupervised. The outcome of this work was the so-called Basle Concordat of 1975, which defined the division of responsibilities between parent and host authorities in supervising banks' foreign establishments. The second main area on which the Committee's work focused was the introduction of supervision of individual banks on a worldwide consolidated basis, covering not only the activities of the domestic head offices but also those of their foreign affiliates wherever they might be located.

It is fairly clear that in the present environment of rapid change and internationalization the main challenge for regulatory authorities will be the harmonization of national frameworks and, as far as possible, the formulation of an international approach with regard to instruments and techniques. International efforts to harmonize banks' capital requirements illustrate the direction of present regulatory activity.

In 1985 the European Council endorsed the objectives and timetable proposed by the Commission for the completion of the internal market. In 1986 the Treaties establishing the EEC were supplemented by the Single European Act, which strengthened the legal and procedural instruments for achieving EEC objectives, and in February 1987 a Directive implementing the first stage of the liberalization of capital movements came into effect. The programme for the liberalization of financial services envisages full freedom of establishment, endorses the principle of supervision by the country of establishment and distinguishes between matters to be dealt with by 'harmonization' and those amenable to 'mutual recognition' of countries' different rules. Care will no doubt have to be taken to ensure that the latter does not give rise to any risk of rules gravitating towards the standard of the least demanding country.

6.4   The Effectiveness of Monetary Policy

Deregulation and financial innovation can have many different effects on the relationship of changes in the money stock to inflation rates, real economic growth rates and interest rates, which may have important implications for the conduct and effectiveness of monetary policy based on quantitative monetary targets. The demand for traditional means of payment may be reduced by innovations which facilitate transactions. In some countries the introduction of interest payments on transactions balances has made it more difficult to identify transactions money and, along with the payment of market-related interest rates on savings instruments, has altered the way the aggregates respond to changes in interest rates. Traditional indicators of liquidity (the extent to which an instrument can be sold or redeemed at short notice at minimum cost and without significant loss) have also in many cases become less meaningful. In fact, widespread use of marketable instruments tends to blur the distinctions between the money, credit and capital markets and, together with the availability of contingent instruments may ultimately call for a redefinition of the concept of liquidity. Innovations which enable banks to economize on reserve holdings can influence money supply relationships as well as the demand for money. Increased competition in the financial sector, which tends to reduce the cost of intermediation, has at times encouraged simultaneous expansion in the borrowing and liquid-asset holdings of non-financial entities. International integration of the financial markets, which greatly facilitates the shifting of liquid balances by large corporations, in particular, between jurisdictions and in response to interest rate and exchange rate movements, could in time further reduce the stability of the demand for national monetary and credit aggregates. International banks can, with a stroke of the pen, transfer domestic liabilities to their offshore books and vice versa. Offshore deposits might, in principle, be incorporated in the money stock, but in practice delays in the availability of the data have in most cases precluded this.

Problems of this kind have been more acute in some countries than in others. In most countries that employ monetary aggregates as targets or indicators the concepts or definitions have had to be changed in recent years to accommodate financial innovation. Yet when large changes in the financial system take place it may take time to establish the behaviour of newly defined aggregates. Increasingly, too, it has become necessary to monitor items such as offshore deposits and contingent positions which are excluded from the principal aggregates. In the UK the objectives for broad money have been abandoned, but in Germany, France, the Netherlands, Spain and Greece problems caused by financial innovation have so far not proved insurmountable. In some of these countries the use of new short-term marketable instruments, such as CDs or commercial paper, which have recently been authorized, has so far remained limited, but it could increase as market infrastructures develop or in the context of a change in interest rate expectations. In several EEC countries, of course, the anti-inflationary monetary policies pursued in recent years have been based mainly on efforts to maintain stable exchange rates within the EMS. But such an approach does not resolve the problems associated with monetary targeting since there remains the question of what can be used as an anchor for price stability in the system as a whole. The anchor has so far been provided, in effect, by a relatively high degree of price stability in one member country which employed a monetary target. One quetsion for the future is whether some other kind of anchor would be more appropriate once the planned liberalization of exchange controls opens the way to potentially larger and more volatile capital flows. Looking further ahead, moves towards creating an integrated financial market in the EEC raise fundamental questions about the kind of monetary policies and institutions which may be needed, assuming that the aim is to achieve a high degree of stability in the exchange rates between members' currencies.

With respect to the techniques of implementing monetary policy, central banks have responded to innovation in the money markets and have indeed sought to foster it by adopting more flexible market-oriented instruments. To complement the outright sale and purchase of securities, extensive use has come to be made of securities repurchase agreements and swap transactions in the foreign exchange market for supplying bank reserves and influencing money market interest rates in very flexible ways.

Gradual but substantial changes in monetary policy transmission mechanisms have also been taking place. The liberalization and development of the markets enables interest rate impulses deriving from changes in monetary policy to be transmitted more rapidly through the financial system, though their effect may be attenuated by portfolio adjustments. The availability of floating interest rates and hedging instruments may weaken the traditional effect of changes in interest rate on the timing of investment in real estate and industrial equipment. But while the impact of monetary policy on new savings and investments decisions may be blunted it will affect existing financial positions. In fact, over time, the transmission of monetary policy impulses has increasingly come to rely less and less on credit squeezes caused by credit-rationing effects and more on the effects of interest rates on overall spending. Whether this means that larger changes in interest rates are needed than in the past to achieve a given effect on spending is debatable.

The greater pervasiveness of price mechanisms, together with interest rate flexibility, may mean that a given rise in interest rates will have a broader impact on the cost of servicing outstanding debt. The use of long-term instruments with floating interest rates may have tended to stabilize interest rates on outstanding debt in real terms at times when shifts in nominal interest rates mainly reflected unpredictable changes in inflation rates. It may therefore have protected borrowers against excessive changes in the real interest cost of outstanding debt. The situation may be different in the context of a relatively stable price level, in which changes in interest rates mainly reflect real shocks, or in circumstances in which inflationary pressures begin to build up. To the extent that rises in interest rates affect not only potential new borrowers but also those with outstanding debt, there is some risk that unwelcome distributional effects and the possibility of insolvencies among the banks' customers could undermine the readiness or ability of the monetary authorities to tighten monetary policy should a rise in interest rates become necessary to counter a build-up of inflation.

A similar risk may be involved in the extensive use of instruments such as NIFs and other standby credits, since, in the event of a pronounced tightening of market conditions and a concomitant widening of the interest margins of intermediation, banks might all simultaneously be called upon to honour their commitments. The resulting overcrowding of their balance sheets with paper or credits of this kind – probably mostly issued by major, prime customers – could tend to have a twofold effect. First, it could crowd out smaller customers with no such back-up or standby facilities at their disposal, resulting in an inequitable sharing of burdens and of the sectoral impact of policy restraint. Second, if interest rates had to rise more than before to achieve a given restrictive effect, an increase in interest rate volatility over the cycle might also have undesirable allocative and distributive effects as well as tending to destabilize exchange rates. Moreover, because of the potential solvency implications, such price effects of monetary policy might adversely influence the stability of the financial system as a whole. In short, the existence of a large number of credit and standby commitments might render the active use of monetary policy more costly, less effective and politically less acceptable. Of course, for most countries these are only potential problems, since the various credit enhancement techniques are not yet widespread enough to constitute a risk on any appreciable scale. Even so, developments in the main centres may be indicative of the directions in which the financial system is moving.

In any case, internationalization of the financial markets and greater asset substitutability seem bound to narrow the scope for discretionary interest rate policy in individual countries. Short-term interest rate policy in many countries has been increasingly pre-empted by exchange rate considerations in recent years, and even in the largest countries interest rate changes have increasingly been reflected in movements in exchange rates. In these circumstances changes in the monetary policy stance could tend to have relatively more impact on the international trading sector of the economy and relatively less on domestic investment. This might not be welcome when the disturbances with which monetary policy has to cope originate in the domestic economy. Given that prices in the goods and labour markets adjust more slowly than prices in the financial markets, uncoordinated implementation of changes in national monetary policy can lead to large exchange rate movements in real terms. The resulting swings in international competitive positions could tend to discourage investment in the internationally traded goods sector and to encourage protectionist trends. Hence there is a risk that in the absence of international coordination of monetary policies, integration in the financial sector could lead to disintegration, or at least to a lesser degree of integration, in the real sector of the world economy. The need for greater international coordination of monetary policies in the interests of greater stability in the exchange rate relationships between the currencies of the largest countries was recognized at the Plaza meeting in September 1985 and in the Louvre Accord in early 1987.

7 CONCLUSIONS

While financial innovation has undoubtedly helped to reduce the cost of financial intermediation and to improve certain aspects of allocative efficiency, it has given rise to a number of problems. Lack of transparency, underpricing, over-expansion of new credit lines and greater interest rate and exchange rate volatility may entail economic costs and a risk of instability in the financial system. Central banks and supervisory authorities have already responded to these challenges, but more still needs to be done.

More efficient and pervasive markets may not produce satisfactory results in the presence of regulatory distortions. Many innovations are the product of the desire to circumvent regulations. Not all regulations are dispensable. Increased international harmonization of national regulatory systems is a necessary condition for avoiding distortions caused by innovation.

Unilateral national deregulation, which has been a major influence on the recent wave of innovations, may be considered to be a form of international harmonization to the extent that it removes regulatory biases and distortions. However, there is some doubt as to where competition for larger slices of the international financial business cake may eventually lead. In some areas rules are still required whereas in others innovation calls for new ones. A supra-national approach is needed to avoid competitive distortions and would also help to ensure the stability of the financial markets and the international system. There is always a risk that, as a result of competitive pressures, business will gravitate towards areas that are least regulated, even though individual banks tend to welcome rules which limit abuses engendered by myopic behaviour and the fight for market shares.

More generally, greater openness and financial market freedom, which are both a cause and a result of innovation, call for greater caution, judgement and responsibility on the part of market participants. Regulation, by nature, tends to lag behind market developments: it should not seek to be too detailed or comprehensive and it can never be a full substitute for responsible individual behaviour. Whether the present wave of innovations will in the long run increase the stability of the financial markets and their potential for benefiting the economy, therefore, will in large measure depend on the behaviour of the major market participants – notably the banks and other financial institutions themselves.

7

Financial Innovation and Capital Formation

José Viñals and Angel Berges

In recent years, Western countries have undergone an intense process of financial innovation which has changed quite fundamentally – and in some instances perhaps lastingly – the functioning of their financial markets. Although this has generated an abundant literature on the factors causing financial innovation, and its effects on financial stability and monetary policy effectiveness,[1] it is not clear, however, how much all these financial developments have influenced the real sector of the economy, namely production, saving and investment decisions.

This issue is likely to remain controversial in the near future for the following reasons: first, the difficulty of giving a precise definition of what is meant by financial innovation, since this encompasses not only new financial instruments but also changes in the very nature of financial markets due to securitization, global integration, etc.; second, the lack of a well-defined conceptual framework that clearly establishes the linkages between financial innovation and production, saving and investment decisions; finally, the scarcity of solid empirical evidence on the effects of financial innovation on the real sector of the economy.

The above problems notwithstanding, the more modest aims of this chapter are to provide a relatively simple conceptual framework that can be used to think about the effects of the new financial instruments on capital formation, and to assess

[1] See, for example, Dufey and Giddy (1981), Mayer (1982), Silber (1983), Van Horne (1985), BIS (1986) and Kaufman (1986).

how important these effects have been in Europe. Given that since the mid-1970s European economies have experienced what are generally agreed to be disappointingly low rates of investment, and given also that a sustained increase in the rates of private investment on plant and equipment is seen as a most important requirement to move to a faster growth path and better employment conditions in Europe, it seems of great policy relevance to analyse how the new financial instruments can be expected to influence, if at all, decisions regarding the volume and composition of private capital formation.

The chapter is organized in five sections. Section 1 examines the true meaning of financial innovation, and the conditions under which its effects spill over to the real sector of the economy. Section 2 looks at the various theoretical determinants of private investment, and discusses how important they are likely to be in practice. Section 3 surveys the most significant new financial instruments and analyses their potential and actual contribution to investment financing. Section 4 focuses on the recent changes observed in the financial behaviour of European firms to see if they can be related to the emergence of the new instruments. Section 5 ends the chapter with a summary of the main conclusions obtained and with a discussion of the main implications for financial policy.

1 FINANCIAL INNOVATION: ITS NATURE AND MEANING

Financial markets have become a key element in the functioning of modern economies. In turn, the existence of financial markets themselves can be traced back to two elements: time and uncertainty.

Regarding the time dimension, saving and investment decisions are made by households and firms after solving complex constrained multi-period optimization problems. Thanks to financial markets, they are allowed to transfer purchasing power from the present to the future and vice versa in such a way as to allow saving to be channelled into the most profitable investment opportunities. A simple example can show how economic agents benefit from the intertemporal reallocation of resources made possible by financial markets.

Consider an individual who lives over two periods (today, 1, and tomorrow, 2) and who is endowed with $(\bar{y}_1, \bar{y}_2)$ quantities of good y in each period, as represented by point E in figure 7.1. It is clear that if the individual does not do any investment, his consumption possibility locus will equal the area defined by the $0\bar{y}_2E\bar{y}_1$ rectangle. Alternatively, the individual may choose to invest part of his current income (y_1) in return for a larger amount of future income (y_2). This, in turn, results in an enlargement of the consumption possibility locus to the area inside $0DE\bar{y}_1$ in the figure. How does the existence of financial markets change the situation? Figure 7.2 represents the case where the individual can lend and borrow at rate r in the financial market. Here, the optimal thing to do will be to invest up to point B, where the rate of return of investment – given by the slope of the ED curve – just equals the cost of capital (r). By following such a strategy, figure 7.2 shows that, as a result of the existence of financial markets, the consumption opportunity set of the individual is increased by the shaded areas to 0FBG.

Regarding the uncertainty dimension, the presence of risk in economic life can be a serious impediment to the efficient allocation of resources unless there exists a complete set of contingent commodity markets. However, as shown by Arrow (1964) and Debreu (1959), even when the number of available markets is smaller than the number of contingent commodities (which equals the number of goods times the number of states of nature: $n \times s$), an efficient allocation of resources is made possible by the existence of enough financial instruments.[2] Specifically, there will be an efficient allocation of resources through the market whenever the number of independent marketable securities equals the number of states of nature (s). In such cases, it will be possible to exactly reproduce the allocation of resources obtained with $(n \times s)$ contingent commodity markets by instead purchasing appropriate amounts of the (s) distinct securities, each of which pays a given sum of money when a particular state of nature occurs, and then using the proceeds to

---

[2] This assumes perfect foresight regarding future spot commodities prices.

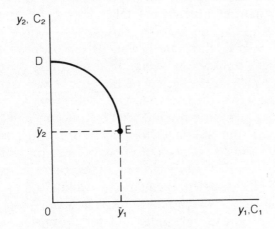

Figure 7.1   No financial markets.

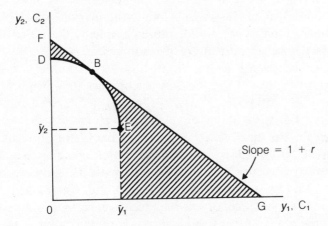

Figure 7.2   Financial markets.

buy the desired quantities of goods in the (*n*) spot markets available. In sum, in an uncertain world a complete set of financial markets is critical to the achievement of an efficient allocation of resources.

In reality, nevertheless, financial markets seem to be quite different from the above ideal cases in several important respects.

First, financial markets are incomplete, in the sense that the number of financial instruments falls short of the number of contingencies; as explained above, this leads to serious economic inefficiencies. Second, there are operational inefficiencies associated with the high transaction costs of channelling savings into investment, which are reflected in the gap between the return most individuals earn on assets and the cost they pay as borrowers.

In short, the lack of many financial instruments and imperfect functioning of the markets for many existing instruments produces an unsatisfied demand for financial services which, when appropriately satisfied, can yield economic profits. Therefore, as Levich (1987) has stressed, the market is willing to pay for those financial innovations which reduce the transaction costs of doing things that are already possible, and for those which allow a better spread of risk in the economy by allowing people to do things they could not do before. In this respect, Van Horne (1985) has proposed to define as financial innovations all those new products or processes that 'make the markets more efficient in an operational sense and/or more complete', therefore helping to achieve a better allocation of resources.

It may be useful to recall at this point that the financial innovation process does not only encompass new products (e.g. interest rate futures) or new processes (e.g. electronic fund transfers), but also major changes taking place in the financial framework. In a recent study, the Bank for International Settlements (BIS, 1986) listed these major changes as: (1) the trend towards securitization associated with the growing role of capital markets to the detriment of credit markets; (2) the increasing importance of off-balance-sheet activities by banks; and (3) the global integration and internationalization of financial markets. Keeping this in mind, the definitional criterion for financial innovation can be usefully applied to the debate about whether such innovations are no more than a zero-sum game played exclusively within the financial sector and leading merely to an increasing number of transfers and transactions without benefiting the real sector of the economy or whether, on the contrary, such innovations spill over to affect favourably real economic decisions like saving, investment and production. In this regard, those things which are sold in the market as financial innovations but which do not either lower financial transaction costs and/or contribute to a better spreading of risks, will not have favourable effects either on the operational efficiency and/ or completeness of financial markets. Consequently, they will not help – but may actually hurt by diverting scarce resources from truly productive activities – the real sector of the economy. As indicated by Van Horne (1985), Miller (1986) and the BIS study (1986) among others, this is not to say, though, that there will not be accounting profits for those introducing the pseudo-innovations, at least until the market finally recognizes that nothing really new is being offered.

In the sections that follow, rather than trying to answer normative questions regarding economic welfare, we focus on the more limited but still important positive issue of how the recent wave of innovation in financial instruments can affect private capital formation.

2 ECONOMIC AND FINANCIAL DETERMINANTS OF INVESTMENT

It is a firmly established fact that the rate of capital formation is a key element in determining the growth rate of the economy. Nevertheless, when studying the effects of financial innovation on capital formation it is best to distinguish between the long term and the short term.

In the long term, competitive profit-maximizing firms have a demand for capital that depends on the costs of capital and the other factors of production. Assuming, for simplicity, that there are only two factors, capital (k) and labour (l), in equilibrium each factor's marginal product will be equal to its marginal cost. Taking (r, w) to be respectively the real cost of capital and labour, and assuming a well-behaved linear homogeneous output (y) producing technology $y = f(k,l)$, the labour and capital demand schedules for the typical firm – easily obtained from the marginal conditions – are k^d (r_-,w_+) and l^d (r_-,w_+) respectively. Therefore, the long-term capital stock demanded by the typical competitive firm will go down whenever the rental cost of capital increases, and will go up whenever the cost of labour goes up, in proportions that critically depend on the specific form of the production technology, $f(.)$, used by the firm.

So far, we have just looked at the partial equilibrium situation represented by the typical firm. It is also important to explore what will happen to the long-term capital stock of the economy (the aggregate[3] of each firm's capital stock) whenever there is a change in its relative cost. To find out, it is necessary to bring in the general equilibrium conditions – supply equals demand – in goods and factor markets.

In the (stationary) long-term situation, factor market equilibrium is represented by conditions $K^d(r_-,w_+) = K$ and $L^d(r_-,w_+) = \hat{L}$. Assuming that the total labour force ($\hat{L}$) and the cost of capital are given,[4] both equations can be solved for the two unknowns (K,w) allowing us to obtain the long-term reduced form expression for the capital stock, $K(r_-,L_+)$. Consequently, changes in the cost of capital or the labour force will affect the economy-wide capital stock in a way that depends crucially on the aggregate technology of the economy.

Given that some of the new financial products are usually credited with lowering the financial cost of capital to firms, it is clear how the new financial instruments could affect the long-term capital stock of the economy through this channel. Since the aggregate capital stock depends negatively on the cost of capital, a drop in this cost will raise the capital stock in a proportion that depends on the production technology of the economy. To get an idea of the order of magnitude involved, it may be useful to take a stylized example not too far removed from reality. In the case of a Cobb–Douglas, constant returns to scale, production function with a share of labour in total income of two-thirds, the elasticity of the long-term aggregate capital stock of the economy with respect to the rental cost of capital is 1.5. That is, a 1 per cent reduction in the cost of capital increases the long-term capital stock of the economy by 1.5 per cent, which is a very substantial effect.

It would be inappropriate, however, to conclude from the above that cost of capital reduction induced by financial

---

[3]Firms are taken to be identical to avoid aggregation problems.

[4]For example, in a small open economy the rental cost of capital is given by the rest of the world.

innovation will have as great an effect on investment in the short to medium term, which is the horizon most relevant for policy purposes. The basic reason – supplied by the modern theory of investment developed by, among others, Jorgenson (1963), Eisner and Strotz (1963), Lucas (1967), Gould (1968) and Treadway (1969) – is that capital is durable and firms are subject to increasing costs when changing the capital stock. Therefore, firms will carefully take into account the present and expected future consequences of adding a new unit of capital before embarking on a new investment.

More formally, a competitive firm invests (I) so as to maximize its own value (V) subject to the constraints imposed by technology (f), the capital stock adjustment[5] costs [$C(I/K)$], the dynamics of capital accumulation, and financial costs (ρ). That is[6]:

$$\max V_t = E_t \left\{ \sum_{j=0}^{\infty} \beta^j [f_{t+j}(K_{t+j}) - C_{t+j}(I_{t+j}/K_{t+j}) - I_{t+j}] \right\}$$

subject to:

$$K_{t+j} = (1-\delta)K_{t+j-1} + I_{t+j},$$

where: E_t is the expectational operator conditional on information available at time t; $\beta^j = \pi^j_{s=1}(1+\rho_s)^{-1}$ is the discounting factor dependent on the real financial cost of capital (ρ) to the firm (π being the product operator);[7] and, finally, δ is the rate of depreciation of the capital stock.

Calling q the shadow price associated with the capital accumulation restriction,[8] the derived investment equilibrium condition is that the firm will invest up to the point where the increase in its value due to an extra unit of capital just equals

[5]These costs are generally specified to be quadratic and convex.
[6]To simplify, variable inputs are maximized out, the price of capital and output are equal, and taxes are not taken into account.
[7]The explicit formula for β^j is:

$$\beta^j = \pi^j_{s=1} \ (1+\rho_s)^{-1} = (1+\rho_1)^{-1}(1+\rho_2)^{-1} \ldots (1+\rho_j)^{-1}.$$

[8]The q variable mathematically corresponds to the multiplier associated with the capital accumulation constraint. When solving the first order conditions of the maximization problem, we find that the firm's q equals:

$$q_t = E_t \left[\sum_{j=0}^{\infty} \beta^j \frac{\delta Z_{t+j}}{\delta K_{t+j}} (1-\delta)^j \right],$$

where $Z_{t+j} = f_{t+j}(K_{t+j}) - C_{t+j}(I_{t+j}/K_{t+j}) - I_{t+j}$.
Therefore, q will be higher when: the financial cost of capital is lower (β higher), when the net income (Z_{t+j}) coming from the addition to the capital stock is higher and when the rate of depreciation of the capital stock (δ) is lower.

the marginal cost of purchasing and installing the unit. Therefore, if the purchase of the unit of capital costs one unit of output, and the marginal installation costs are $C'(I/K)$ units while the firm increases its value as a result by q units, then it must be that $1 + C'(I/K) = q$. This expression can also be rewritten as $I/K = h(q-1)$, $h'>0$, which is nothing but the popular Tobin's q theory of investment.

According to Tobin's q theory, investment depends positively on the present discounted value (to the firm) of the extra unit of capital (q). In turn, q will be larger when the 'marginal efficiency of capital' (i.e. the stream of expected earnings generated by the extra unit of capital) is higher, and when the financial 'cost of capital' to the firm (i.e. the discount rate used in the present value calculation) is lower. As a result, when firms have ready access to external finance (debt and equity) as well as to internal finance, their investment decisions will be fully determined by the evolution of q dictated by the behaviour of the marginal efficiency of capital and the cost of capital. Consequently, new financial instruments which (a) change the financial cost of capital to the firm, (b) help the firm cover contingencies or (c) provide new and more flexible financial arrangements, will affect investment by affecting q. While the first effect works through the cost of capital channel, and the third through the marginal efficiency of capital channel, the second works through both channels.[9]

Finally, there is another channel through which new financial products may have an effect on investment in addition to the

---

[9]The traditional derivation of the investment function assumes that there are no uncovered contingencies or that only expected values matter for the firm's investment decision. Given that it would take too long to fully derive a model of investment that explicitly accounts for risk, we simply assume that anything that gives better risk-hedging opportunities to the firm improves q. As an example, in a mean-variance framework the risk-adjusted q would be equal to the q we have been using so far, minus the product of the extra risk introduced in the earnings and financial costs of the firm by the new investment, multiplied by the cost of risk, as perceived by firm's owners. Therefore, the larger is this risk, or its cost to the firm, the lower will be the risk-adjusted q, as shown in Nickell (1978, ch. 8, pp. 160–5). In this case, financial innovations that provide coverage of risks to firms have the effect of increasing the risk-adjusted q, by allowing firms to 'sell' their risk in the market at a price lower than their cost of risk. In what follows, we implicitly take the marginal efficiency of capital, and the cost of capital to be on a risk-adjusted, or certainty-equivalent basis. See also Fazzari et al. (1987) for a modification of the traditional investment model that incorporates financial market imperfections.

'profitability' q channel. This happens whenever financial market imperfections make firms' investment decisions depend on their financial structure.

The issue of the relationship between investment and financing decisions has been a controversial one in the financial literature for the last thirty years. The debate, too well known to reproduce at any length here, started with Modigliani and Miller (1958) showing that, under the assumption of perfect capital markets and given the firm's investment policy, financial structure is irrelevant to the value of the firm. Most of the following controversy has centred on how financial structure can become relevant – even if investment policy continues to be exogenously given – due to market imperfections.[10] Our main interest here, rather, is on those financial market imperfections which make investment decisions depend on financing decisions.

The most important of these imperfections is the asymmetry of information between providers and users of funds, which can cause severe financial constraints to the firm.[11] Given that potential suppliers of funds cannot always distinguish 'good' from 'bad' firms, new shareholders and debtholders will want to be compensated for any losses made from inadvertently financing 'bad' firms by charging all firms a premium to cover possible losses. This will then increase the cost of external finance to the firm. At the same time, recent work regarding the existence of asymmetric information in loan markets shows that if lenders are unable to distinguish 'good' from 'bad' borrowers they will behave optimally by setting credit limits (see Stiglitz and Weiss, 1981).

The above problem has quite unfavourable implications for the ability of modern firms to make the types of investment that the changing industrial structure demands. On the one hand, small and new firms – probably the most dynamic and adaptable to changing industrial demands – are most likely to face financial constraints or higher costs due to the difficulties they have in

[10]Among the imperfections considered, are corporate taxes (Modigliani and Miller, 1963), bankruptcy costs (Scott, 1976; Kim, 1978), Haugen and Senbet (1978) or personal taxes (Miller, 1977).

[11]See the articles by Myers (1976), Greenwald et al. (1984), Myers and Majluff (1984) and Fazzari et al. (1987).

showing the market how good they are. On the other hand, high-technology firms, and in general firms intensive in tangible assets, also face large informational asymmetries, as well as uncertainty regarding the liquid value of assets in the event of bankruptcy. As Long and Malitz (1986) have shown, they are also likely to suffer from severe external financing constraints.

In sum, when asymmetric information prevails in financial markets firms may suffer from external financial constraints and limited opportunities for substituting debt for new equity. This is consistent with firms' investments depending not only on the existence of good profit opportunities (reflected in q) but also on the availability of internal finance. In this regard, a variable such as current profits or cashflow, which proxies for internal finance conditions, may also be an important determinant of investment. An implication of the above is that new financial instruments that alter the degree of informational asymmetry in financial markets, or have an impact on the current profits or cash flows generated by firms, will also affect investment.

2.1   *Empirical Evidence Regarding Investment Equations*

Before drawing any conclusions about the overall effects of financial innovations on investment, it is necessary to review the evidence regarding the effects of q and financial constraints on investment. Table 7.1 (pp. 170–71) summarizes in chronological order several of the most relevant recent empirical studies on investment functions for the US, major European countries and Japan. The main conclusions we reach after looking at the international evidence, both at the aggregate and firm level, are the following: first, the q-channel is not very significant in explaining investment behaviour, the effects of q on investment being generally small and slow; second, those studies which separate the marginal efficiency of capital from the cost of capital components of q find that the first component generally has larger and more significant effects on investment than the second;[12] and third,

---

[12]This is done explicitly in Abel and Blanchard (1986). The studies by Mairesse and Dermont (1985) and Bruno (1986) also distinguish between profit and cost of capital effects, finding that the second is not generally statistically significant.

variables such as current profits, cash flow and sales also seem to matter for investment, often dominating the role of q.[13] To summarize, figure 7.3 (p. 172) graphically illustrates the main determinants of investment and their empirical role.

In sum, the lessons we learn from the theoretical and empirical literature on investment reviewed in this section are the following: while the new financial instruments are likely to have only a limited effect on investment by lowering the cost of capital to the firm, they may nevertheless have a significant effect on investment by helping firms' profitability, and by relieving their financial constraints.

3   AN ANALYSIS OF THE NEW FINANCIAL INSTRUMENTS

Having defined in the previous two sections the nature and meaning of financial innovation and the main economic and financial determinants of investment, we now analyse in detail the new financial instruments and how they can contribute to investment. This contribution can be in terms of: (1) making available new external financial sources previously unavailable to firms (financial constraint effect), (2) providing cheaper sources of investment finance (cost of capital effect) or (3) allowing the firm a better financing of working capital, or a better covering of the risks arising from investment or financing decisions (efficiency of capital and cost of capital effects).[14] To complete the analysis, we also examine how large these potential effects are likely to be, given the actual use firms make of the new instruments, and given the relative size of the latter in financial markets.

It must be pointed out that any review or classification of innovations in financial instruments risks omitting some which may be of interest to market participants. Our purpose here,

[13]See for example Mairesse and Dermont (1985), Chirinko (1987) and, especially, Fazzari et al. (1987).

[14]An example of risk arising from investment decisions would be when an investment project yields an output whose price is uncertain. An example of risk arising from financing decisions would be a firm suffering from exchange rate risk and/or interest rate risk as a result of financing the investment project through certain channels.

Table 7.1 Recent empirical evidence on investment equations

Studies	Country	Data	Main findings
Abel (1980)	US	Aggregate	The elasticity of investment to q is significant and ranges between 0.5 and 1.1
Meese (1980)	US	Aggregate	Insignificant relative price effects, very significant lagged dependent variables
Summers (1981)	US	Aggregate	q has extremely low effects
Hendershott and Hu (1981)	US	Aggregate	Insignificant effects of the cost of capital on equipment investment
Chappell and Cheng (1982)	US	Firm	q not significant
Salinger and Summers (1983)	US	Firm	q significant in half the firms
Poterba and Summers (1983)	UK	Aggregate	Very mixed results
Mairesse and Dermont (1985)	France Germany US	Firm	Current and past output, and profits, have significant effects; not very significant effect of the cost of capital

Study	Country	Level	Results
Dinenis (1985a,b)	UK	Aggregate	Current and past q have significant effects on investment
Abel and Blanchard (1986)	US	Aggregate	q significant but: large, serially correlated residual, the marginal efficiency of capital component has larger and more significant effects than the cost of capital component, profits and output variables also matter
Chirinko (1986a)	US	Aggregate	Even when separation between structure, equipment and inventories is made q-effects are still extremely low, lagged variables matter and there is serial correlation of residuals
Bruno (1986)	a	Aggregate	Large effects of profits, insignificant effect of the cost of capital
Chirinko (1987)	US	Aggregate	Very small q-effects, serial correlation, cash flow enters but not robust to estimation technique, past investment and current output also have important effects
Hayashi and Inoue (1987)	Japan	Firm	Significant but very weak effect of q; profits and past values of q also matter
Fazzari et al. (1987)	US	Firm	Investment sensitive to q but also to cash flow in firms likely to be financially constrained

a Bruno (1986) runs *ad hoc* investment equations for US, Canada, Japan, UK, France, Germany, Italy and Sweden.
Source: Most of the studies are discussed in Chirinko (1986b).

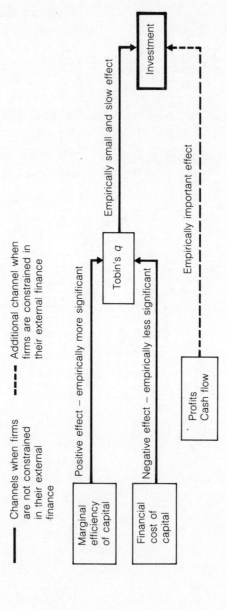

Figure 7.3 The determinants of capital investment.

however, is not to give an exhaustive coverage of all the new financial instruments, their origin, or degree of success,[15] but rather to focus on those which – at least potentially – are more closely related to investment decisions of non-financial firms.

Our analysis takes as its starting point the distinction usually made in corporate finance theory between debt and equity as the available sources of external finance to the firm. As is well known, debt and equity differ in terms of the kinds of financial obligation they impose on the firm. While straight debt implies payment obligations which are invariant with respect to both the firm's performance and future financial conditions, equity, on the other hand, allows much more financial flexibility to the firm, since it is paid out of the funds remaining after the firm has met all its contractual costs.

This simple but theoretically attractive distinction can be used to classify the main new financial instruments as in table 7.2. The first three categories of instrument in the table represent recent modifications of traditional debt and equity instruments to finance investment, while the last includes those instruments which facilitate the coverage of investment or financing risks. Each of these categories of new financial instruments is discussed in detail in what follows.

3.1 Special Debt Instruments

The first group in this category – floating interest rate debt instruments – includes those instruments whose financial charges are not fixed in advance but rather vary according to financial market conditions. Floating rate debt instruments were originally introduced in the early 1970s by financial institutions seeking to avoid interest rate risk in a period of increased volatility in financial markets. The first major development was the generalization of variable rate loans (VRLs), especially in the Euromarkets. In this type of loan, the interest paid by the borrower is the sum of some known spread plus a variable base interest rate representative of the financial institution's cost of

---

[15]For an analysis along those lines see Dufey and Giddy (1981), Silber (1983), Van Horne (1985) and BIS (1986).

Table 7.2 Classification of the main financial innovations

Special debt instruments
Variable rate loans
Floating rate bonds ⎫ Floating rate debt
Note issuance facilities ⎭

Zero-coupon bonds ⎫ Special fixed rate debt
Junk bonds ⎭

Leasing

Debt–equity hybrid instruments
Convertible bonds
Bonds with warrants
Prêts participatifs

Special equity instruments
Euro-equities
Venture capital

Risk-covering instruments
Swaps
Futures/forward rate agreements
Options

---

financing. The use of variable interest rates has also extended more recently to bond issues (floating rate notes or FRNs), where the interest payment is also linked to some representative base interest rate.[16]

A mixture of the two instruments just described (VRLs and FRNs) are the so-called NIFs or note issuance facilities, probably one of the clearest signs of financial innovation in the present decade. NIFs are basically equivalent to commercial paper programmes with the added feature that a financial institution guarantees the borrower the availability of short-term financing (three to six months) over a medium-term (five to seven years)

---

[16]A special form of this last instrument is the perpetual FRN, whereby the principal is never recovered; interest is paid, on a floating basis, forever.

horizon. The paper issued by the borrower is either placed with investors (similar to FRNs) or kept by the guaranteeing institution (similar to VRLs). Interest payments of NIFs are generally linked to the interbank rate, usually with a discount since NIFs are issued by high-quality borrowers with sometimes even better risk-ratings than many banks.

Having briefly reviewed the nature of the main floating debt instruments, we now focus on how they can potentially contribute to capital formation through any of the three channels previously mentioned.

By their very nature, floating rate debt instruments do not provide completely new sources of finance, although they have a comparative cost advantage with respect to previously existing financial sources. On the one hand, relative to traditional long-term (straight) debt, they have the cost advantage embedded in the liquidity preference hypothesis: average expected costs of short-term financing are generally found to be lower than known average long-term costs. Moreover, they constitute a particularly attractive source of financing whenever a firm's revenues are positively correlated with interest rate movements (i.e. due to the inflation component of both nominal interest rates and cash flows, etc.). On the other hand, relative to straight short-term debt, floating rate debt is, in principle, equivalent, in terms of finance availability, to the rolling-over of short-term debt. Nevertheless, there are two important advantages to the former. First, by receiving the guarantee that finance will be available in the future – at the then prevailing market interest rates – the firm avoids the risk of being rationed out of the credit market in the future. Second, even if there were no future credit rationing, the cost of short-term financing to the firm may still increase if its credit rating deteriorates. This risk is avoided with the new instruments since the spread (or discount) is usually set in advance for the entire life of the instrument.[17]

To summarize, it seems that floating rate debt instruments can be potentially very useful to finance working capital at lower costs – which increases the net profitability of the firm for any

---

[17]In NIFs, however, banks usually have the right to opt out if a borrower's credit standing deteriorates.

Table 7.3 Flow of funds raised in the international financial markets (US$ billion)

Country	1984				1985				1986			
		Eurobonds				Eurobonds				Eurobonds		
	VRL	TOTAL	FRN	NIF	VRL	TOTAL	FRN	NIF	VRL	TOTAL	FRN	NIF
West Germany	—	2.1	1.0	—	—	3.2	0.9	0.3	—	11.1	1.0	—
France	2.0	8.5	5.4	0.6	4.0	11.4	6.4	2.7	3.6	13.4	4.0	2.5
UK	3.4	5.0	3.7	0.7	5.1	15.3	12.1	3.3	2.2	19.0	12.4	9.8
Italy	4.7	3.7	3.5	0.2	4.7	5.2	4.2	1.0	6.0	5.4	2.0	1.4
Spain	3.5	1.7	1.0	0.7	2.5	1.4	1.1	0.4	4.4	1.7	1.4	1.3
Netherlands	0.3	1.1	—	—	0.3	1.4	0.1	1.4	0.5	2.8	—	0.9
US	5.3	25.0	5.5	2.3	3.1	40.5	10.5	15.0	4.7	44.7	10.7	5.9
Total	19.2	47.1	20.1	4.5	19.7	78.4	35.3	24.1	21.4	98.1	31.5	21.8

VRL: variable rate loans
FRN: floating rate notes
NIF: note issuance facilities
The total amounts shown correspond to the countries listed and may differ from world totals.
Source: Euromoney Syndication Guide.

given investment project – and also to finance physical investment projects whose returns are closely correlated with interest rates. In terms of the main determinants of investment discussed in section 2, the existence of floating interest rate instruments can help increase a firm's q by increasing the marginal efficiency of capital and by lowering the financial cost of capital.

But to assess how important these q-type effects are likely to be in practice, we must first answer two questions: how large is the size of the market for the new instruments relative to the overall market for financial sources, and how much are these instruments used by non-financial corporate borrowers as opposed to financial institutions themselves.[18] If the answer to both questions is favourable, then it is important to ask whether there really has been a lowering of financial costs as a result of using the new instruments relative to the previously existing ones. We now address these questions subject to the constraints imposed by data availability.

Starting with market size, most of the available data correspond to international financial markets. Table 7.3 summarizes the volume of funds raised by borrowers in the major European countries and the US between 1984 and 1986. As observed, bank lending in variable terms has grown hardly at all in the last three years, while the issues of Eurobonds have more than doubled, and those of NIFs are now more than four times larger than in 1984. Nowadays, total variable rate international financing (VRLs + FRNs + NIFs) represents almost 10 per cent of the total financing sources available in each of the European countries considered except in the UK, where the figure goes up to 15 per cent. Regarding NIFs alone, they represent about 1 per cent in each of the European countries studied, except in the UK where they represent 3 per cent.

One may wonder how much these numbers change when we add to the international market data the national market data. The answer is that generally they do not change much, at least

---

[18]Interbank dealings of some instruments can also have an effect on investment, as long as they allow financial institutions to lower their costs, and the savings are passed on to the firms. This channel seems a much more indirect way of providing finance to firms.

Table 7.4 Worldwide commercial paper (issues outstanding at the end of 1986 in US$ billion)

Market	Volume
US	323.0
Canada	11.4
Sweden	7.4
Spain	5.4
Australia	4.3
France	4.0
Hong Kong	1.2
UK	1.0
Other countries	1.3
Subtotal	359.0
Euromarkets (NIFs)	35.0
Total	394.0

Source: Bank of England (1987a)

for those instruments for which we have been able to find data.[19] Table 7.4 shows an estimate of the worldwide volume of commercial paper issues outstanding at the end of 1986. Among the EEC countries only Spain, France and the UK have a domestic commercial paper market, and only in Spain does its volume represent a significant share (5 per cent) of the total flow of funds of the economy. But to make things even worse, it is not only the case that the market size of the most dynamic new variable rate debt instruments (FRNs and NIFs) is small. It also happens that they are used to a large extent by the financial institutions themselves as a way of finding resources. As table 7.5 shows, more than half of the FRNs issued in international

[19]Although we have not found internationally homogeneous data on domestic VRLs for the European countries studied, it seems that they form about 80 per cent of total loans in countries such as Italy, France and the UK, according to Akhtar (1983). Regarding FRNs, the figures are 80 per cent of total bond issues for Italy, and 20 per cent for France, with no figures for other European countries.

Table 7.5 Financial institutions' share of total FRNs and NIFs (% issued in international financial markets)

	1982	1983	1984	1985
FRNs	38.8	25.0	42.8	52.7
Total bonds	15.3	16.5	21.4	26.4
NIFs	29.3	53.9	17.1	27.5

Source: BIS (1986)

markets in 1985 were issued by banks. Most of the rest were issued by governments, while firms continued issuing mainly fixed interest rate bonds. On the other hand, the banks' share of NIFs issued has fluctuated from 29.3 per cent in 1982, to 53.9 per cent in 1983 and back to 27.5 per cent in 1985. Nevertheless, since according to the BIS (1986) study, at most 20 per cent of the total NIFs arranged have actually been drawn, this means that NIFs are mainly used as a back-up facility and not as a direct source of funding. As a result, this makes their effective use by firms as a method of finance far lower than the table suggests.

In sum, the limited evidence available seems to indicate that floating rate bonds and NIFs generally play a minor role in the financing of non-financial corporate institutions. On the other hand, the outlook does not seem too optimistic when we look at price rather than quantity data. To take an example, in the discussion of the new financial instruments of the variable interest rate category, NIFs were singled out as being potentially very useful as a source of financing to firms. But if we look at figure 7.4, which shows the average discount in NIF rates with respect to the interbank rate, it can be seen that it goes down from more than 1.2 per cent in 1980 to virtually zero in 1985. We interpret this as indicating that as the increase in NIFs issues took place in the period (table 7.3) lower-quality borrowers came to the market, wiping out the financial cost-advantage of NIFs relative to traditional sources of finance. Because of both the very low market size of NIFs in European countries and their vanishing

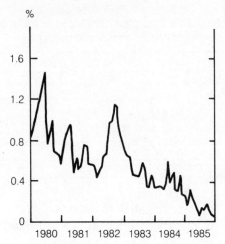

Figure 7.4 Three-month London interbank bid rate less ninety-day commercial paper.
Source: Euromoney Syndication Guide.

cost advantage, we conclude that this new instrument has had in general a minimal effect on the financing of firms. Variable rate loans, on the contrary, seems to be quite important in size – if one adds to the international issues the domestic issues – and greatly used by firms (see footnote 19).

Our main conclusions regarding the potential and actual contribution of floating rate debt instruments to investment are summarized in the first three rows of table 7.6.

A second class of special debt instruments included in table 7.2 are pure fixed interest rate debt instruments issued either with a very delayed or flexible repayment schedule, or with a high subordination to other debt issues, so that their risk characteristics are more like those of equity. A typical example of the first are zero-coupon bonds. These are medium- to long-term bonds without any interest or principal payment before maturity. The return to the investor (cost to the issuer) comes from the difference between the face value of the bond (to be returned at maturity) and the issuing price. Such absence of intermediate payments makes this type of instrument very attractive to finance investment, especially in heavy industries or research-oriented ones with a long maturity period before investments start paying back. However, despite the apparent

Table 7.6 The new financial instruments and investment

Type of instrument	Economic contribution to investment[a]			Usable/ used by firms[b]	Practical importance[c]
	1	2	3		
Variable rate loans		x	x	s	s
Floating rate bonds		x	x	w	w
NIFs/commercial		x	x		
paper				w	w
Junk bonds	x		x	w	w
Zero-coupon bonds	x		x	s	w
Leasing	x		x	s	s
Convertible/warrants		x	x	s	w
Participating loans	x		x	s	w
Euro-equities		x		s	w
Venture capital	x			s	w
Swaps	x	x	x	s	s
Futures – FRAs/			x		
options				w	w

[a] 1 Offering finance not previously available
    2 Previously available finance, but at cheaper cost
    3 Adding flexibility or hedging facilities for financial obligations.
[b] The extent to which main users are firms as opposed to financial institutions.
[c] Weight of the particular instrument in total European non-financial business finance.

In both [b] and [c], s and w indicate strong and weak respectively.

attractiveness of this option, there seems to be little evidence of these instruments being used in most European countries (see Morgan Guarantee Trust, 1986).

Without doubt, the most representative exponent of low-grade (or no grade at all) debt issues are the junk bonds used in the US mainly to finance leveraged take-overs. Their ultimate goal, very often unrelated to the financing of real investment,[20] and their virtual absence in the European financial markets mean that junk bonds can be expected to have little impact on helping finance European (or US for that matter) investment.

A final type of special debt instrument detailed in table 7.2 is leasing. Although it has been around too long to really be considered as a recent financial innovation, its relation to real investment is, nevertheless, probably the closest of all the instruments considered so far. This is because virtually 100 per cent of the finance provided by leasing is tied to the use of physical equipment (which is not acquired and financed, but rather leased). The way leasing helps investment is by creating a source of finance that was previously unavailable. Additionally, it is a flexible source, not in relation to the repayment schedule – which is fixed in advance – but in the sense that it does not alter the borrowing capacity of the lessee as long as neither the equipment nor its associated liabilities appear in the financial statements.

Table 7.7 shows the importance of leasing in the total capital formation of the major European countries, as compared to the

Table 7.7 Penetration of leasing in capital formation[a] (1982 data, %)

Country	Penetration
Germany	3.0
France	8.5
UK	13.0
Italy	6.8
Spain	4.5
Netherlands	5.1
Europe	6.9
US	27.9

[a] Leasing investments as a percentage of total capital formation.
Source: OECD (1986)

[20]Although it is true that junk bonds are most often used for leveraged buy-outs, it might still be argued that the increased risk of take-overs – caused by the existence of junk bonds – can discipline managers in their search for the optimal investment policy.

US. The average for Europe is close to 7 per cent, much smaller than the 28 per cent of the US, but definitely larger than all the financial innovations considered so far.[21] It must be noted here that an additional, although hard to quantify, advantage of leasing over the other instruments is that while only a few large and highly rated companies can have access to most financial innovations, leasing is available to virtually every manufacturing company, regardless of size or age. The corresponding rows of table 7.6 summarize the probable contribution of special fixed interest rate debt instruments and leasing to investment.

3.2   Debt–Equity Hybrid Instruments

A large number of financial instruments, mostly in the form of securities, have been developed with some mixed features between debt and equity financing. This category of instruments can be characterized as adding flexibility to the financial obligations of the issuing firm. They are issued formally as debt but their remuneration incorporates some features which allow them to enjoy some equity advantages.

The main exponents of hybrid instruments are convertible bonds and bonds with equity warrants. The difference between them is that convertibles disappear after conversion, whereas a bond with an equity warrant can remain as a straight bond after the warrant is exercised. In both cases, the bond carries a given interest (usually fixed) lower than the equivalent on a similar straight bond. This lower interest is compensated for by the possibility of realizing important capital gains at conversion, or warrant exercise.

In studying how these instruments can help investment through the three channels mentioned at the beginning of the section, it can be seen that both convertibles and warrants have several interesting features. On the one hand, they provide finance similar to that provided by straight debt but at a lower cost.[22] On the

[21]Although the available data relate to 1982, more recent but fragmentary data from the Bank of England indicate an increasing role for leasing between 1982 and 1986.

[22]This is so initially since the total implicit cost can be larger if conversion causes a large earnings dilution. This is the reason why, in the corresponding row of table 7.6 columns 2 and 3 have been marked, although, in practice, only one will apply depending on the conversion exercise.

other hand, if the bond is converted into equity, the new financial obligations for the firm are much more flexible than before. Finally, in certain cases, they may allow indirect equity financing to firms that otherwise might find it difficult, or impossible, to raise equity financing in the stock market. This last aspect is, however, somewhat doubtful since unlisted (in stock exchanges) firms could hardly place convertibles or bonds with warrants given that the conversion or exercise is usually dependent upon the issue's stock prices. For these reasons, such hybrid instruments can only expect to play a significant role in firms' financial sources when they are backed by a deep and liquid stock market.

According to the data in table 7.8 this is not the case in most European countries (except in the UK). As shown, total stock market capitalization in the European countries listed is, on average, about 20 per cent of GNP, compared to the 50 per cent of the US. Also, less than 20 per cent of the securities outstanding are traded in a full year. If we add to this that the securities issued by financial institutions represent a large fraction of both market capitalization and trading, and consider the heavy market concentration in the largest companies, there is actually little scope for the use of hybrid securities (or even pure equity financing) by a wide range of non-financial companies.

Table 7.8 National stock markets comparison (year 1985, %)

	Trading as % of market value	Market value as % of GNP	Market concentration[a]
Germany	20	21	45
France	n.a.	14	24
UK	30	58	28
Italy	10	15	54
Spain	10	10	52
Netherlands	25	25	n.a.
US	40	50	15

[a] Percentage of total market value accounted for by the ten largest listed companies.
Source: Euromoney Syndication Guide and OECD (1986)

Table 7.9   Hybrid instruments issued in the international financial markets (US$ billion)

	1984	1985	1986
Convertibles	4.2	4.6	6.5
Bonds with warrants	2.6	2.7	15.3
Convertible and warrant bonds; breakdown by issuing countries			
Germany	0.1	0.4	1.8
France	0.1	0.2	0.6
UK	0.3	0.6	1.4
Italy	0.0	0.1	0.8
Spain	0.0	0.0	0.0
Netherlands	0.1	0.0	1.1
US	2.0	1.7	13.4

Source: Euromoney Syndication Guide

Actual data on convertibles and warrant issues are only available for the international financial markets, and are shown in table 7.9. It may seem at first sight that bonds with warrants are at present expanding rapidly in the world. However, the increase in the quantity of warrant issues in 1986 is mostly due to Japanese institutions, stimulated by the recent Tokyo Stock Exchange boom. Also, a breakdown of issuing activity by European countries shows how insignificant is the market size for convertibles when compared to other sources of finances, such as floating debt instruments (shown in table 7.3) or looked at in relation to total financial needs. Once again, the evidence seems to indicate the very small role of the new financial instruments in financing investment.

In addition to convertibles and warrants, there is another hybrid instrument with a virtually nil degree of use. The *'prêt participatif'*, introduced first in France and then in Spain, is a mixed debt–equity instrument whose remuneration consists of a fixed part (debt-feature) plus a variable part linked to some measure of the earnings of the borrower. Since it has seldom been used other than as a substitute for former problem loans to almost bankrupt firms (and in many instances has been imposed as the only alternative to a complete default) it can hardly be considered as an important financial innovation regarding investment.

The corresponding rows of table 7.6 summarize the probable contribution of hybrid instruments to investment.

3.3 *Special Equity Instruments*

This category of instruments refers to those forms of equity which are issued outside traditional stock exchanges. Two main types of instrument of a very different nature can be included in this category, as seen in table 7.2.

The first are the so-called Euro-equities, whereby large and well-known firms place shares in different countries, not through the stock markets, but through the underwriting and placing network of the Euromarkets. In terms of the three channels outlined above, the potential influence of Euro-equities on investment is clearly in terms of reducing the cost of financing. It cannot be considered as providing a previously non-existent financing source because what the issuer gets is simply pure equity denominated in its own currency. By issuing it in several markets, however, the firm can have access to a wider spectrum of investors without lowering its share price too much (which would be equivalent to raising the cost of capital). An idea of the practical importance of the Euro-equities market is given by the fact that the volume of issues has grown up considerably from some $200 million in 1983, when they first started, to over $7 billion in 1986. Unfortunately, however, the number of companies benefiting from this new instrument is very small, with a dozen large European companies tapping over 70 per cent of the market. It seems, therefore, that access is restricted to large and well-known companies (Fiat and KLM are the largest issuers so far).

A completely different story lies behind the second special equity instrument: venture capital. Contrary to Euro-equities, it was originally designed to meet the financing needs of new and small companies unable to issue equity in traditional stock markets. None the less, the high risk involved in investing in shares of new and little-known small companies – usually with not much more than 'good ideas' as assets – makes it necessary to have some sort of government support for the development of the venture capital market. In most European countries, this support has been either of an institutional or a fiscal type. The first type is exemplified by the starting of parallel or unlisted security markets to provide liquidity for ventures. The second involves granting some kind of fiscal relief on the return obtained by venture capital investors. It is also quite common to provide venture capital in complex packages, including some loans, particularly managerial support agreements, to help reduce the uncertainty and lack of information faced by investors.

Despite the efforts made by most European governments and the potential attractiveness of venture capital markets in providing a new form of finance not previously available, its actual penetration is still extremely low. As table 7.10 indicates, for the EEC as a whole venture capital represents 0.2 per cent of GNP; that is, one-hundredth of the value of stock market capitalization shown in table 7.8. Even in the US, where it started five years earlier, it is no more than 0.4 per cent of GNP. Consequently, venture capital markets have played a minor role in the financing of European – and US – investment.

Table 7.10   Availability of venture capital (year-end 1984)

	US$ billions	As % of GNP
Germany	0.25	0.04
France	0.15	0.03
UK	3.0	0.70
Italy	0.15	0.04
Spain	0.08	0.01
Netherlands	0.55	0.5
EEC	.4.3	0.2
US	15.0	0.4

Source: Financial Times

The corresponding rows in table 7.6 summarize our views on the role of the special equity instruments in financing investment.

3.4   Risk-Covering Instruments

The final class of innovations considered in this section are those capable of facilitating hedging against risk. In this group we include swaps, financial futures (and forward rate agreements) and options.

The first types of instrument to consider are swaps. Taken to be one of the main examples of financial engineering, swaps are a technique whereby two parties agree to exchange two streams of interest payments. These can be: (1) in the same currency but with a different interest rate base (interest rate swap, for example between a fixed rate and a variable rate base interest payment); (2) in the same base interest but in different currencies (currency swap); or (3) in different base interests and different currencies (cross-currency interest rate swap). Consequently, swaps are not only risk-covering instruments, but also true sources of finance as long as they enable the borrower to raise funds in the market in which he has a comparative advantage – i.e. due to some kind of market segmentation – and swap the proceeds into his preferred type of liability.

It can be concluded, therefore, that swaps have the potential to stimulate investment. Specifically, swaps can give (indirect) access to a given financial source which was not available before; they may reduce the cost of previously available financial sources;[23] and, finally, they can provide hedging for interest rate and/or exchange rate risk.

Turning to the data, it must be noted that measuring the volume of swap markets, or the degree of involvement of non-financial firms, is an almost impossible task as a whole chain of interbank operations can develop between two end-users, and as banks are not required to report regularly their swap activities (off-balance-sheet). All the available statistics are purely esti-mations, like those shown in table 7.11. As can be seen, in the five years of market existence in currency swaps, the volume has

---

[23]This is so as long as the two parties share the total cost saving produced by the swap operation, which is not uncommon.

Table 7.11 Estimated volume of the swap market (US$ billion)

	Interest rate swap (outstanding notional value)		Currency swaps (flows)
	Dealer–end user	Dealer–dealer	
1982	3	n.a.	3
1983	20	n.a.	6
1984	80	n.a.	13
1985	142	28	24
1986	250	57	45

Source: Bank of England (1987b)

skyrocketed especially in interest rate swaps, where outstanding notional value has grown by a factor of 100. These figures should be treated with caution, however, as in interest rate swaps there is no exchange of principal but only of the associated interest payments, while in currency swaps it is not uncommon to exchange the principal.

Perhaps the most interesting aspect of table 7.11 is that dealer–dealer swaps – the interbank portion of the swap market – only represent about 20 per cent of the total market. This is not to say that all the remaining volume has gone to finance non-financial firms, since end-users can also be financial institutions. But with no alternative evidence it is not possible to deny that swaps may actually be used to finance real investment either. In addition, the story told by the trend in the average swap spread relative to the Treasury bond yield shown in figure 7.5 seems somewhat more encouraging than in the NIF case. Despite the tremendous increase in swap market activity in recent years, spreads have only slightly increased from around 0.8 per cent in early 1984 to around 1–1.1 per cent at the end of 1986. Extrapolating the trend, we conclude that the market could still allow a good deal of lower-quality new borrowers before spreads go up substantially, therefore eliminating the cost-advantage of swap operations.

Figure 7.5 Five-year Treasury bond yield and five-year swap spread, daily data, April 1984–September 1986. [a]Five-year swap price (pay fixed versus six-month Libor) minus five-year Treasury bond yield.
Source: Bank of England Quarterly Bulletin, February 1987

The two other financial innovations available to facilitate hedging are financial futures and options. In a futures contract, buyer and seller agree to exchange a pre-specified amount of the underlying asset at a given future date at a price set on the day the contract is agreed. An essential aspect of the futures trading mechanism is the role of the Clearing House as intermediary between the buyer and the seller. Another is the marking-to-market, whereby the value of the outstanding contract is adjusted daily to movements in futures prices. These two aspects facilitate the cancellation of contracts prior to their expiration date by simply entering a reverse contract. The extension of futures trading to financial instruments was initiated in Chicago in 1975 and today it covers a wide range of financial instruments (as underlying assets) among which Treasury bonds and bills, Euro-dollars, stock indexes and the major currencies account for over 90 per cent of the total (financial) futures market share, well ahead of traditional commodity futures.

An option, on the other hand, gives the holder the right, but not the obligation, to buy (call option) or sell (put option) a pre-specified amount of the underlying asset at a pre-determined price within a given period. The trading mechanisms are very similar to those in futures markets and, apart from the heavy and well-established – especially in the US – trading of options on shares, the main underlying financial assets are the same as for the financial futures.

Let us now turn to the issue of investment and how financial futures and options can help to finance it. As is clear from the description of these instruments, they do not directly contribute to the generation of new or cheaper financial sources for firms. Because futures and options are traded only in secondary markets, they cannot be used as a source of funds for any type of borrower. The only possible way of directly influencing investment is through the risk reduction obtained by hedging against adverse interest rate or exchange rate movements.

To get an idea of how important this effect is likely to be, we look now at market size. As table 7.12 shows, the size of the financial futures and options markets has increased dramatically during the present decade, both in terms of open interest (market value of outstanding contracts) and trading volume. How much of that volume is risk-covering and how much is speculation is difficult to calculate as most exchanges do not receive any information about the basic purpose of entering a contract. There is, however, some indirect but indicative evidence that can be obtained by simply relating the open interest and trading volume data shown in the table. Open interest indicates the market value of all contracts existing at a given point of time (year-end, in table 7.12), and is a stock-type measure. Trading volume indicates, on the other hand, the average daily purchases, and sales, of contracts at market value, and is a flow-type measure. Dividing the latter measure by the former we obtain an estimate of the liquidity of the market, given by the percentage of existing contracts that change hands daily. Conversely, dividing the stock (open interest) by the flow (daily trading volume), we obtain an estimate of the average holding period of a contract. When such calculation is done, it turns out that the average holding period is three to four days, which can hardly be thought of as a reasonable

Table 7.12   Volume of major financial futures and options markets
(US$ billion)

	Open interest			Daily trading volume		
	1980	*1985*	*1986*	*1980*	*1985*	*1986*
Futures	81	254	440	25	86.	135
Interest rate	79	236	412	24	73	116
Stock index	—	10	18	—	9	14
Currency	2	8	9	1	4	4
Options	—	138	240	—	24.5	16
Interest rate	—	89	162	—	11.5	6.7
Stock index	—	37	39	—	12	15.6
Currency	—	12	39	—	1	2.5
Total futures and options	81	392	680	25	111	169

Source: Levich (1987).

period for hedging purposes. Therefore, speculative activity seems to be very important in the market.

Alternatively, the obtained average holding period can be compared to the average time to maturity of the contracts being traded at any moment. In the futures market, the nearby contract (the one with heaviest trading volume in most cases) expires, on average, within forty days, whereas the other contracts expire after more than forty days; therefore it is probably not erroneous to think that much less than 10 per cent of the contracts are kept until maturity.[24] Since hedging with a futures contract is only perfect if it is held until maturity, it can be concluded that the risk-hedging element of futures contracts is not large.

[24]This reasoning cannot be readily applied to American options, since they can be exercised at any time prior to maturity.

Therefore, the effective length of contracts for these instruments suggests that they are not greatly used by firms to reduce the uncertainty surrounding their investment decisions.

A risk-covering instrument similar in many regards to financial futures is the forward rate agreement (FRA), whereby two parties (mainly banks) agree on the interest of a (notional) deposit to be made at a future date. Given that they are tailored to meet the two parties' needs regarding both the quantity and the future date of the contract, FRAs have more flexibility for hedging purposes than futures, where both the quantity and maturity date of the contract are set by the Futures Exchange. The actual use of FRAs as hedging instruments by firms can, however, also be considered as marginal, with a total estimated trading volume in international markets of one-hundredth that of the interest rate futures, and most of it being of an interbank nature according to BIS (1986). The last rows of table 7.6 summarize our views about the effects of risk-covering instruments on investment.

3.5 Summary

Having reviewed in this section the potential usefulness of the new financial instruments in stimulating capital formation (columns 1, 2 and 3 of table 7.6), their relative importance in overall financial markets and their use by firms (the last two columns of table 7.6), it is our impression that, among them, only variable rate loans, leasing and swaps are likely to have any significant effects. Moreover, as the evidence contained in table 7.1 and figure 7.3 on the main determinants of investment indicates, the role of these financial innovations will be more significant whenever they help increase the profitability of the firm, e.g. by providing better hedging devices, or make available external financial sources not previously available that relieve the financial constraints suffered by firms. As columns 1 and 3 of table 7.6 show, one or both of these features seem to be present in the three instruments singled out. On the contrary, the other instruments reviewed do not seem to have the capability or market size to play a significant role in influencing investment, at least up to the present date.

Table 7.13 Internal and external finance structure of non-financial companies (%)

	Total debt[a] (Total liabilities)		Long-term debt[a] (Total debt)		Direct debt[a] (Total debt)		Internal finance[b] (Total sources)	
	1975	1985	1975	1985	1975	1985	1975–80	1981–85
Germany	57.1	56.0	33.8	28.6	n.a.	n.a.	68.3	81.1
France	70.0	69.9	25.3	26.2	2.3	2.5	47.3	38.6
Italy	68.4	67.8	37.3	34.2	1.0	2.1	23.8	23.9
UK	52.1	54.6	21.4	15.3	16.7	8.9	52.6	55.9
Netherlands	55.3	56.2	45.7	39.5	8.5	1.7	53.1	71.4
US	34.3	40.5	54.1	54.2	34.3	30.4	57.2	68.1

Source: OECD Non-financial Companies' Financial Statements

a Outstanding liabilities in balance sheet.
b Flow of finance raised on average during the period.

Data on Spain were not available before 1982.

4   RECENT FINANCIAL BEHAVIOUR OF EUROPEAN FIRMS

So far, we have discussed how the new financial instruments can make a potential contribution to the financing of real investment by firms. In addition, we have examined the extent to which each of these instruments is significantly used by firms. To complete the analysis, we now look at the recent financial behaviour of European firms to see if it is possible to identify any aggregate effects related to the emergence of the new instruments.

Table 7.13 presents information about changes in the financial structure of European and US non-financial companies over the 1975–85 period. The first two columns show the weight of debt finance in total liabilities, and the other pairs of columns indicate the share of long-term debt (over 18 months) in total debt, the percentage of total debt raised directly in securities markets, and the dependence of firms on internal, as opposed to external, finance.

From this body of data it is possible to draw the following conclusions: (1) contrary to what one would expect, the recent wave of innovation in financial instruments has not made European – or even US – firms more dependent on external finance, but has had rather the opposite effect – except in the case of France, in the European countries considered firms have increasingly relied on internal finance;[25] (2) the new instruments have not altered significantly the debt–equity ratios of European firms in the aggregate, in contrast to the US where they have gone up; (3) except in the case of France, there has been a shift from long- to short-term debt in the financial structure of European firms, which contrasts sharply with the stability shown in the US; this can partly be explained by the lower inflationary expectations held in the mid-1980s, which may have induced

---

[25]This holds true despite the fact that the OECD data used show no clear trend in profitability (measured by the net earnings/equity ratio) when comparing the 1975–80 and 1981–85 periods. Therefore, the increased role of internal finance cannot be satisfactorily explained by an increase in profits alone.

firms to borrow either in long-term variable interest rate debt, or in short-term debt. The more active substitution of variable for fixed long-term debt in the US relative to European financial markets can explain the US–Europe contrast; (4) the securitized part of the debt is still extremely small in European firms' balance sheets, in clear contrast to the US; moreover, in the UK – where financial innovation has been more intense than in the rest of Europe – and in the Netherlands, an increasing fraction of debt has been raised through financial intermediaries, rather than directly in securities markets; (5) although debt–equity ratios have remained very stable, the fact that this has happened together with an increase in internal finance, all of which goes to increase equity, implies that external equity issues have lost importance in the financing of European firms. At the same time, it is rather striking that this has happened during a period of both financial innovation and booming stock market prices.

In short, although it is dangerous to draw causal implications, it seems that the emergence of the new financial instruments has not been accompanied in Europe by an increasing accessibility to firms of external finance sources, or to securities markets, or by substantial modifications of debt–equity ratios. At the same time, the reduction in the average maturity of the debt of European firms indicates the relatively small substitution of variable for fixed long-term debt. Undoubtedly, the new financial instruments must have resulted in some changes in the relative importance of specific debt and equity instruments in their respective debt and equity totals. However, it does not look like the development of these new instruments has been accompanied by major changes in the financial structure of European firms. If anything, European firms seem at present to be more dependent on internal finance and on intermediated external finance than they were ten years ago.[26]

It is of interest to note that all the above facts are consistent with the conclusions reached in section 3, which indicated the

---

[26]In fact, the weight of internal sources in financing physical investment (that is, netting out of investment the acquisition of financial assets), is actually larger than it appears from table 7.13. Mayer (1987) estimates the percentage of internal sources used in the financing of physical investment for the period 1970–84 to be 62 per cent in France and 101 per cent in the UK.

relatively low importance of the markets for the new financial instruments in Europe, and the little use that was made of them by European firms in many cases. Therefore, although the discussion in that section indicated that the new financial instruments had the potential to grant firms better access to external finance, it is not clear that they have made a major contribution to the relaxation of financial constraints in the European non-financial corporate sector.

5 CONCLUSIONS AND POLICY IMPLICATIONS

The recent wave of financial innovation taking place in Europe is generally credited with increasing the efficiency of financial markets and, often, with facilitating the channelling of saving into the most profitable investment opportunities. In spite of all this, the rates of investment of most European countries continue to be much lower than what is judged to be desirable.

In this chapter, we have explored the relationship between innovation in financial instruments and capital formation, placing special emphasis on the European context. The main questions raised and discussed have been whether there are any channels through which the new financial instruments may affect investment, whether these channels are wide enough in practice and whether innovation in financial instruments has been a sizeable phenomenon in Europe. Our tentative answers are affirmative in the first case, only partially so in the second and negative in the third.

Although it is true that all of the new financial instruments reviewed have the potential to affect real investment decisions either by making available to firms cheaper or more flexible external finance sources, or by allowing them better cover against financing- or investment-related risks, the available empirical evidence indicates that these potential effects have not been very important in practice. There seem to be two main reasons why this has happened: on the one hand, the empirical evidence on investment functions suggests that new financial instruments that mainly reduce the cost of capital to a firm are likely to have a very limited impact on that firm's investment in the short to medium term, whereas the opposite seems to be the case for those new instruments that help relax the firm's external financial constraints; on the other hand, even for the last types of instrument, it is often the case that they are neither very significant, in terms of market size, nor much used by firms. Among the instruments reviewed, only variable rates loans, swaps and leasing operations seem to meet all the requirements to make them useful for firms' investments.

Overall, the development of the new financial instruments has not been reflected in an increased accessibility to European firms of external finance, in a reduced dependence on intermediated debt or in marked changes in debt–equity ratios. On the contrary, these firms seem to be at present generally more dependent on internal finance, and on intermediated external finance, than they were ten years ago. Consequently, European firms do not seem to have benefited much so far from the increasing availability of new financial products, at least as regards the financing of assets.

The implications for financial policy are several. First, policy-makers must realize that many of their moves to deregulate and free financial markets may lead mainly to a proliferation of interbank transactions, and to secondary market and speculative trading, without really helping firms to finance their investment projects. Second, given that the problem with many of the new instruments is not lack of potential for helping firms with their investments, but rather one of market size and low use by firms, there seems to be some room for financial and tax policies in helping to promote the growth of the potentially most useful markets. This seems to apply most of all to products, such as venture capital, which can best meet the financing needs of small and new firms, high-tech firms and generally those firms investing in intangible assets. A final implication is that, if the ultimate main problem is how to promote investment, there is perhaps much more that could be done through appropriate macro-economic supply and demand policies than through financial policy.

Finally, we must insist that our tentative conclusions refer only to the new financial instruments, not to the financial innovation process itself. At the same time, it must be noted that, since financial innovation has supplied savers with a wider array of assets and firms with more effective cash management techniques, this may have led to changes in the saving rate of the economy, and in the mix between the physical and financial investments of firms, which may have also affected investment. In addition, many of the interbank transactions observed in the market may have improved risk spreading and lowered costs within the banking sector which, in turn, may have benefited more recent borrowers through the lower cost of new and traditional credit lines. These issues, which exceed the scope of this chapter, are important enough to warrant careful future investigation.

REFERENCES

Abel, A.B. (1980) Empirical investment equations: an integrative framework. *Carnegie–Rochester Series on Public Policy*, 39–91.

Abel, A.B. and Blanchard, O.J. (1986) The present value of profits and cyclical movements in investment. *Econometrica*, 249–73.

Akhtar, M.A. (1983) Financial innovations and their implications for monetary policy: an international perspective. BIS Economic Papers no. 9.

Arrow, K.J. (1964) The role of securities in the optimal allocation of risk-bearing. *Review of Economic Studies*, 91–6.

Bank of England (1987a) Commercial paper markets: an international survey. *Quarterly Bulletin*, 46–53.

Bank of England (1987b) Recent developments in the swap market. *Quarterly Bulletin*, 66–79.

BIS (1986) *Recent Innovations in International Banking*. BIS, Basle.

Bruno, M. (1986) Aggregate supply and demand factors in OECD unemployment: an update. *Economica*, suppl., 35–53.

Chappell, H.W. and Cheng, D.C. (1982) Expectations, Tobin's *q*, and investment: a note. *Journal of Finance*, 231–6.

Chirinko, R.S. (1986a) Investment, Tobin's *Q*, and multiple capital inputs. Working Paper no. 2033, National Bureau of Economic Research.

Chirinko, R.S. (1986b) Will the neoclassical theory of investment please rise? The general structure of investment models and their implications for tax policy, mimeo, University of Chicago.

Chirinko, R.S. (1987) Tobin's *q* and financial policy. *Journal of Monetary Economics*, 69–87.

Debreu, G. (1959) *Theory of Value*. John Wiley, New York.

Dinenis, E. (1985a) Adjustment costs, Q, taxation, and investment in the UK. Discussion Paper no. 235, Centre for Labour Economics, LSE.

Dinenis, E. (1985b) Q, gestation lags and investment: is the flexible accelerator a mirage? Discussion Paper no. 236, Centre for Labour Economics, LSE.

Dufey, G. and Giddy, I.A. (1981) Innovations in the international financial markets. *Journal of International Business Studies*, 33–51.

Eisner, R. and Strotz, R.H. (1963) Determinants of business investment. *Commission on Money and Credit Impacts of Monetary Policy.* Prentice-Hall, Englewood Cliffs, NJ.

Fazzari, S., Hubbard, R.G. and Petersen, B.C. (1987) Financing constraints and corporate investment, mimeo.

Gould, J.P. (1968) Adjustment costs in the theory of investment of the firm. *Review of Economic Studies*, 47–55.

Greenwald, B., Stiglitz, J.E. and Weiss, A. (1984) Information imperfections in the capital market and macroeconomic fluctuations. *American Economic Review*, 194–9.

Haugen, R. and Senbet, L. (1978) The insignificance of bankruptcy costs to the theory of optimal capital structure. *Journal of Finance*, 383–93.

Hayashi, F. and Inoue, T. (1987) Implementing the Q-theory of investment in microdata: Japanese manufacturing 1977–1985, mimeo, Osaka University.

Hendershott, P.H. and Hu, S. (1981) Investment in producers' equipment. In H.J. Aaron and J.A. Pechman (eds), *How Taxes Affect Economic Behavior*, Brookings Institute, Washington.

Jorgenson, D.W. (1963) Capital theory and investment behavior. *American Economic Reivew*, 247–59.

Kaufman, H. (1986) *Interest Rates, the Market, and the New Financial World*. Times Books, New York.

Kim, E.H. (1978) A mean-variance theory of optimal capital structure and corporate debt capacity. *Journal of Finance*, 45–63.

Leland, H. and Pyle, D. (1977) Informational asymmetries, financial structure, and financial intermediation. *Journal of Finance*, 371–87.

Levich, R.M. (1987) Financial innovations in international financial markets. Working Paper no. 2277, National Bureau of Economic Research.

Long, M. and Malitz, I. (1986) Investment patterns and financial leverage. In B. Friedman (ed.), *Financing Corporate Capital Formation*, pp. 325–51. National Bureau of Economic Research, New York.

Lucas, R.E. (1967) Adjustment costs and theory of supply. *Journal of Political Economy*, 321–34.

Mairesse, J. and Dermont, B. (1985) Labor and investment demands at firm level: a comparison of French, German, and US manufacturing, 1970–79. *European Economic Review*, 201–32.

Mayer, C. (1987) New issues in corporate finance. Discussion Paper no. 181, Center for Economic Policy Research.

Mayer, Th. (1982) Financial innovation – the conflict between micro and macro optimality. *American Economic Review*, 29–34.

Meese, R. (1980) Dynamic factor demand schedules for labor and capital under rational expectations. *Journal of Econometrics*, 141–58.

Miller, M.H. (1986) Financial innovation: the last twenty years and the next. *Journal of Financial and Quantitative Analysis*, 459–71.

Miller, M.H. (1977) Debt and taxes. *Journal of Finance*, 261–75.

Modigliani, F. and Miller, M.H. (1958) The cost of capital, corporation finance, and the theory of investment. *American Economic Review*, 261–97.

Modigliani, F. and Miller, M.H. (1963) Corporate income tax and the cost of capital: a correction. *American Economic Review*, 433–43.

Morgan Guarantee Trust (1986) *World Financial Markets*. London.

Myers, S. (1976) Determinants of corporate borrowing. *Journal of Financial Economics*, 147–76.

Myers, S. and Majluff, N. (1984) Corporate financing decisions when firms have investment information that investors do not. *Journal of Financial Economics*, 187–220.

Nickell, S.J. (1978) *The Investment Decisions of Firms*. Nisbet, Welwyn Garden City/Cambridge University Press.

OECD (1986) Financial resources for industry's changing needs. Background Paper, April.

Poterba, J.M. and Summers, L.H. (1983) Divident taxes, corporate investment, and Q. *Journal of Public Economies*, 135–67.

Salinger, M. and Summers, L.H. (1983) Tax reform and corporate finance: a microeconomic simulation study. In M.S. Feldstein (ed.), *Behavioral Simulation Methods in Tax Policy Analysis*. Chicago University Press.

Scott, J.H. (1976) A theory of optimal capital structure, *Bell Journal of Economics*, 33–53.

Silber, W.L. (1983) The process of financial innovation. *American Economic Review*, 89–95.

Stiglitz, J.E. and Weiss, A. (1981) Credit rationing in markets with imperfect information. *American Economic Review*, 393–410.

Summers, L.H. (1981) Taxation and corporate investment: a *q*-theory approach. *Brookings Papers on Economic Activity*, 67–127.

Treadway, A.B. (1969) On rational entrepreneurial behavior and the demand for investment. *Review of Economic Studies*, 227–39.

Van Horne, J.C. (1985) Of financial innovation and excesses. *Journal of Finance*, 621–31.

Index